A Very Special Gift

Nov. 15, 2002

With much love
to
Evelyn and Bill
from

Emily and
Rimer

A VERY SPECIAL GIFT

The Story of the Legacy of

Emily Fisher Crum and

Remer Hamilton Crum

Jaclyn Weldon White

Mercer University Press

MMII

ISBN 0-86554-805-6
MUP/H608

© 2002 Mercer University Press
6316 Peake Road
Macon, Georgia 31210-3960
All rights reserved

First Edition.

Library of Congress Cataloging-in-Publication Data

White, Jaclyn Weldon.
 A very special gift : the story of the legacy of Emily Fisher Crum and
Remer Hamilton Crum / by Jaclyn Weldon White.-- 1st ed.
    p. cm.
 ISBN 0-86554-805-6 (hardcover : alk. paper)
 1. Crum, Emily Fisher, 1914- 2. Crum, Remer Hamilton, 1913- 3. LaGrange College--
Benefactors--Biography. 4. Mercer
University--Benefactors--Biography. I. Title.
 LD2891.L65 W45 2002
 378.758'463--dc21

                                                                    2002009164

This book is dedicated to Thomas Orr Fisher and Bessie Ayers Fisher for their courage, dedication and vision; and to Emily Fisher Crum and Remer Hamilton Crum for their incredible grace and generosity.

CONTENTS

ACKNOWLEDGMENTS

I feel privileged to have been chosen to write this book and I want to thank Marc Jolley and everyone at Mercer University Press for giving me the opportunity to do so. It would not have been possible without Emily and Remer Crum, who so generously shared their time and their memories with me. I'd also like to thank Kirby Godsey, Allen Wallace, Stuart Gulley, Charles Hudson, Dick Gray, Suzanne Harper, Lance Wallace, and Edward Patterson for their invaluable assistance. Finally, as always, I am grateful to my husband, Carl White, for his unwavering love and support.

1. Williford House, Tugalo Street, Toccoa, Georgia

2. Emily and Thomas Williford

3. L-R Sam Fisher, Levi Fisher, T. Orr Fisher,
Masena Fisher, Lois Fisher.

4. T. Orr Fisher

5. T. Orr Fisher and customer, about 1913

6. Bessie Ayers and T. Orr Fisher at Toccoa Falls, Georgia about 1912

7. Bessie and T. Orr Fisher

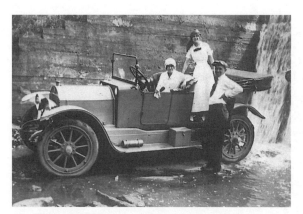

8. L-R Lettie May Ayers, Bessie Ayers, T. Orr
Fisher at Toccoa Falls, Georgia about 1912

9. Bessie Ayers and T. Orr Fisher about 1912

10. Florence Hamilton Crum

11. David A. R. Crum

12. L-R Florence Crum, Remer Crum, Mallette
Crum, Mary Crum, Sarah Crum

13. Emily Crum with
cousin Ernest Ayers, about
1924

14. Fisher Home, North Greenwood Street,
LaGrange, Georgia

15. Remer Crum
about 1938

16. Remer Crum and Emily Fisher, Mexican
marketplace, 1938

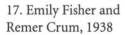

17. Emily Fisher and
Remer Crum, 1938

18. Remer and Emily Crum on their wedding day, 1938

19. Remer Crum in Hawaii, about 1943

20. Emily Crum in Hawaii, about 1943

21. Outside Party, Crum apartment in Hawaii
about 1943

22. Remer and Emily Crum, Christmas in
Hawaii, about 1948

23. L-R Remer and Emily Crum, T. Orr and
Bessie Fisher, Atlanta, Georgia 1966

24. Remer and Emily Crum, Easter, 1966

25. T. Orr and Bessie Fisher on their 50th wedding anniversary

26. Emily and Remer Crum,
Gwinnett County lake house, 1971

27. Remer Crum in the
apple orchard, 1973

28. Ayers descendants at Ayers-Hemphill House, Carnesville, Georgia

29. Emily and Remer Crum, New Smyrna Beach, FL, 1997

30. Emily and Remer Crum, New Smyrna
Beach, Florida, 1997

31. Remer Crum in
his garden, Vinings,
Georgia

32. Fisher-Crum Foundation Meeting, 1998

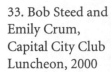

33. Bob Steed and
Emily Crum,
Capital City Club
Luncheon, 2000

34. L-R Dr. Stuart Gulley, Emily and Remer Crum, Dr. Kirby Godsey at Capital City Club Luncheon, 2000

35. Remer Crum and Griffin Bell at Capital City Club Luncheon, 2000

36. L-R Remer Crum, Walter Murphy, Charles
Hudson and Emily Crum at Capital City Club
Luncheon, 2000

37. Wilma Cosper and Emily Crum, Mercer
Trustees Meeting, Sea Island, Georgia 2001

38. L-R Dr. Kirby Godsey, Emily Crum and Remer
Crum, Mercer Commencement 2001

39. Aerial View of Century Center Office Park with boundaries
outlined in white

ONE

A GIFT IS PROPOSED

Stuart Gulley was the first person at LaGrange College to learn about the gift. Although the letter had passed through the hands of his assistant, Lydia Wheitsel, she had been much too busy that late September morning in 2000 to pay attention to the contents. She worked her way quickly through the morning's mail, discarding the junk and setting aside a few routine items she would handle herself. The rest she date-stamped and placed in a neat stack on the president's desk.

Most of the mail was the same sort of correspondence President Gulley received every day. When he came to the letter from the prestigious Atlanta law firm of Alston & Bird, with several pages neatly paper clipped to it, he had no hint of what it might contain. The first sentence removed it from the realm of ordinary mail and almost took his breath away. He slowly read every word of the letter, then turned the same meticulous attention to the attachments. Finally, he set the papers down on his desk and took a few calming breaths, trying to understand the full scope of what he'd just read.

Stuart Gulley had come to this small Methodist college in 1996. He was an ordained minister and had spent ten years at Emory University in a variety of capacities before accepting the top job at LaGrange College. He and his young family had fallen in love with the small town and the school at first sight. Now he sensed he could be on the brink of one of the most memorable moments of his professional life.

He turned his attention back to the letter. It had been written by attorney Benjamin White on behalf of his clients, Emily and Remer Crum, and advised that they planned to make a joint gift of land to LaGrange College and Mercer University. Such a gift from the Crums was not unprecedented. They had, in fact, given land to LaGrange College in the past. What made this proposition so extraordinary was the location of the land they planned to donate. The property in question was the 83-acre Century Center Office Park in Dekalb County, Georgia, and, according to the attached appraisal, it was conservatively valued at $108 million. The potential rental income from existing leases brought the total to $123 million.

President Gulley was quite familiar with Century Center. During his tenure at Emory, he'd attended numerous meetings and functions in the sprawling office park. In his mind's eye, he could see the signature glass buildings, silver-blue against the sky, towering over Interstate 85 north of Atlanta. The magnitude of the proposed gift and what it could mean to his school was difficult to grasp.

The letter requested that President Gulley and other members of his staff attend a meeting on October 11th at Alston & Bird to finalize the arrangements of the donation. President Gulley automatically checked his calendar, but knew there were very few things that could keep him away from that meeting.

A hundred miles to the east, Kirby Godsey, President of Mercer University received an identical letter. He, too, was astonished by the significance of the gift. Although he had guided the school for 22 years, he could not recall the University ever receiving so large a donation. Emily and Remer Crum were warm, caring people who had been engaged in the University's life for a number of years and President Godsey had always found them to be extremely generous patrons of the school. But this gift was so magnanimous, the implications so far-reaching, that he found it difficult to comprehend.

The Crums' proposed gift to these two institutions was so remarkable that it was listed in *The Chronicle of Higher Education* as one of the top twenty gifts to higher education since 1967. Everyone associated with it knew that it was due to the generosity of two wonderful people, but few understood that the seeds of the gift were sown nearly two hundred years before in a tiny northeast Georgia community and nurtured through five generations of a very special family.

Two

The Seeds Are Planted

Robert Hemphill and Henrietta Jenkins were married in Pendleton District, South Carolina in the early years of the nineteenth century, only a few decades after the United States had won its independence. They both came from families who had settled and cleared the area. Like their parents before them, Robert and Henrietta made their living farming. Their first child, John, was born in 1815, followed in two years by daughter Caroline. While there may have been other births, the next child known to have survived infancy was Nancy, born in 1823.

The Hemphills had a good life in South Carolina, living close to family and friends of many years' standing, but Robert Hemphill was very much a product of his generation. The country was new and the mood was one of great possibilities. He longed for fresh frontiers and wanted to know what lay over the next hill. It was not surprising when, only months after the birth of his second son, Samuel, in 1825, Robert and his family loaded all their belongings into a wagon and followed the Old Federal Road southwest into Franklin County, Georgia.

Franklin County had been created in 1784, so it was not a wilderness in 1825, but it was still a remote area of rushing rivers and steeply rolling hills. The Hemphills bought land and built a house on the north fork of the Broad River, a few miles east of the county seat of Carnesville.

While the work of maintaining a farm was hard and the monetary rewards few, the Hemphill family seemed on its way to prosperity. However, their satisfaction in their new home was tempered by the realization that there was a problem with young Samuel. The little boy was physically healthy, but his intellect refused to develop along with his body. Henrietta hoped that he was just a little slower to mature than other children and that time would remedy the situation.

Robert Hemphill did not live long enough to truly enjoy the fruits of his and his family's labor. He died at age 53 in 1828, the same year his last child, also named Robert, was born. Henrietta was left a widow with five children to raise.

They managed well enough, but everyone in the family had to work. Even Samuel was expected to lend a hand with the simpler chores. In 1834, Caroline married Michael Beatenbaugh and the pair moved to his family's farm a few miles away. Six years later, John married Nancy Beard. They built their own house on John's portion of his father's land. Henrietta, Nancy, Samuel and young Robert remained in the original family home.

Henrietta's hopes and prayers that Samuel would outgrow his affliction were to no avail. He was now nearly grown, but his mind was that of a small child and he required constant attention. More and more, as her mother grew older and more fragile, taking care of Samuel fell to Nancy. While Robert was able to help her occasionally, his time was mostly occupied with the work of the farm.

In October of 1859, as the storm clouds of the Civil War were gathering, Henrietta Hemphill died. She was buried beside her husband in the family cemetery. Nancy and Robert were left to run the farm and care for their brother Samuel.

Robert married Mary Bond on July 4, 1861, and brought her to live on the farm with his brother and sister. In July of 1862, their only child, Minnie Tallulah, was born.

The war was now fully underway. John Hemphill joined Company I, 11th Georgia Cavalry and, soon afterwards, his brother Robert followed him into military service. Robert left his wife and sister to manage the farm and cope with the deprivations brought on by the war.

In late November of 1864, he was injured in the Battle of Franklin, Tennessee, and died of his wounds less than two months later. Six years later his wife Mary also passed away. Nancy Hemphill, at age 47, was now responsible for the farm, a brother who needed constant care and a nine-year-old niece.

Gradually the hardships brought on by the war and the resulting reconstruction eased and the farm was prosperous enough to support them. They were able to hire day laborers to handle the heavier tasks. Samuel died in 1875 at the age of 50. Nancy comforted herself with the knowledge that she and her parents had done everything they could to give him a happy life. She and Minnie had grown very close over the years, more like mother and daughter than aunt and niece.

The Hemphill farm was located only a few miles outside of Carnesville. Nancy and Minnie often made the wagon trip into town to shop or attend the Methodist church. It was in Carnesville that Minnie met young Joseph Ayers. They married in 1880, when she was 19 years old, and Joseph moved with his bride into Nancy Hemphill's house.

Joseph's presence made life considerably easier for the two women. Nancy found it a comfort to have a man on the place again. He worked the fields and cared for the animals while Minnie and Nancy handled the never-ending chores in and around the house.

In 1882, Joseph and Minnie's first child, Jeremiah Robert, was born. Clyde Russell and Ernest Joseph followed in 1883 and 1886. The children brought new life and laughter into the old homestead and Nancy began to almost think of them as her own grandchildren.

Whether it was triggered by the births of the children or her own advancing age, Nancy decided the time had come to make her will. Wanting to do everything right, she wrote to Thomas Williford, a lawyer in nearby Toccoa, and asked that he visit and advise her on the writing of her will. He arrived by horse and buggy a few days later.

"I want to leave everything to Minnie's three boys," she told him. "They're my grand nephews—Jeremiah, Clyde and Ernest." She'd given this matter a great deal of thought and was definite about her desires.

Mr. Williford, however, wasn't sure this was the wisest course. He pointed out that Minnie was still a young woman and might very well have other children. Would Miss Hemphill want to leave them out? She had to admit she hadn't considered that possibility. When he suggested making Minnie and her husband the beneficiaries of the will—"Then when they die, everything will go to *all* their children"—Nancy agreed. Mr. Williford prepared the document and, on June 24, 1887, Nancy signed it.

The lawyer's prediction was right on target for Minnie became pregnant again in the early months of 1888. But Nancy would not live to see this fourth child for whom she had provided. She died in May of that year at the age of 65, leaving the farm and the rest of her possessions to Joseph and Minnie.

The Ayers' fourth child, Lucy, was born in November of 1888. Bessie Lois, their second daughter, arrived in 1891 and Lettie May, who quickly became known as May-May, rounded out the family in 1893. The farm flourished and the Ayers family had all the ingredients in hand for a happy life, but tragedy struck within a year. Minnie Ayers had struggled with tuberculosis, known at that time as consumption, for years. When she contracted pneumonia, it was too much for her frail system. She died on September 28,

1894, and was buried in the Carnesville Methodist Church Cemetery.

Joseph now faced a tremendous task. He had six children to raise, ranging from 12 to 1 year in age, and a farm that demanded sunrise to sunset labor, seven days a week. Without Minnie by his side, it seemed impossible. Some changes would have to be made. Joseph came from a big family himself and he knew family was what he needed now.

Several of his seven brothers and sisters lived in Carnesville. Joseph purchased a town lot and began constructing a new house. He knew that, if he lived closer to his family, he could expect help from them with raising the children.

But Joseph himself grew ill before he could finish the new town house. The children cared for him as best they could, but in a world without antibiotics, pneumonia was often a killer. Joseph lost his battle with the disease on May 15, 1895, and was laid to rest beside Minnie. Joseph's brother Sanford assumed the responsibility of running the farm. The six Ayers children, now orphaned, were scattered among their relatives in Carnesville. The boys, old enough to do real work, were the most welcomed. The girls were too young to be of much use and required more care.

Thomas Williford, the lawyer from Toccoa, was Emily Hayes' second husband. She had married Sanford Keeling when she was very young and they'd been an adventurous couple. Shortly after their wedding, they decided to travel west to make their fortune. They'd saved $100 and, as far as they could see, the sky was the limit. They climbed aboard a westbound train, sure that success and riches lay just ahead. But the naïve young couple from North Georgia was no match for the con artist they encountered a few days later. By the time they reached Texas, their $100 was gone, along with the man who'd taken it. Emily and Sanford lived in a railway station for a short time, taking any odd jobs that came along until they were able to save enough for their tickets home. Once back in Toccoa, they settled into a much less glamorous life than the one they'd dreamed of having, but they were safe and secure at home. Keeling died in 1887, leaving Emily a thirty-six-year-old widow. A few years later, she and Thomas Williford married.

When Thomas Williford heard of the misfortune that had befallen the Ayers family, his heart went out to the orphaned children. He and Emily were in their late forties and had no children of their own. They had tried once, a few years before, to take in an orphaned child. The twelve-year-old boy had been abandoned and was living on the streets when the Willifords found him, put him in their buggy and took him home. Emily bathed him while Thomas burned his torn and stained clothes. They bought him clothes and books and special treats, but it was not a happy arrangement from the first. Emily Williford was a woman who demanded obedience and a strict code of conduct. The boy, totally undisciplined, was accustomed to a meaner, less restricted life where he had survived by any means possible.

He began running away. When news that he'd been found reached them, the Willifords would go in their buggy and bring him back home. Life would be quiet and agreeable for a while, then a minor upset would occur and he'd be gone again. Finally, after two or three years of this uneasy existence, they realized something had to be done. One afternoon after bringing him back from another such escapade, the Willifords sat down with the boy in their parlor. Thomas explained the situation as he saw it.

"We love you, son. We'll try to give you everything you want. But you must stop running away. If you leave again, we're not coming after you."

They hoped such straight talk would make him try to behave, but in less than a month the boy was gone again. True to his word, Thomas did not go after him this time. The boy was now fifteen years old and, in that day and time, was considered old enough to make his own way in the world. It wasn't until many years later that they would hear from him, by then a grown man with a family who would thank them for their earlier kindness.

Several years had passed since that failed experiment and the Willifords were moved to try once more to take in another child. They wrote to the Ayers family in Carnesville and expressed interest in taking in one of Joseph and Minnie's little girls. The offer was well received and Bessie, age 4, was chosen to go with the Willifords.

It was a terrifying prospect for a child who'd already endured so much tragedy. Her siblings made it worse by teasing her, telling her that people were coming to take her away and she'd never come back. On the day she was to leave, the little girl was frantic. When the Willifords arrived in Carnesville that blustery November day, Bessie flatly refused to go with these two strangers. She had to be physically carried out of the house, tears flowing freely, and put into the buggy with them.

But the tears soon dried, a result of Emily Williford's soft, soothing words and the cache of presents in the back of the buggy. Bessie had never seen such things. There was a beautifully dressed doll almost as big as she was, and there were bananas, oranges, apples, candy and nuts! When she smiled her sweet smile, the beautiful little brown-eyed girl immediately captured the couple's hearts.

Within days, the Willifords became Auntie and Uncle Tom to Bessie. They spoiled their new ward shamelessly, not only with material things, but also with plenty of love and affection. On Christmas Eve when Bessie was put to bed, the parlor looked as it always did—neat, clean and unremarkable. But when she woke on

Christmas morning, a wonderful transformation had taken place. In the center of the room stood a glorious Christmas tree—the first she'd ever seen—so tall its tip touched the high ceiling. It was decorated with colorful paper chains, glowing candles and popcorn balls, and its evergreen scent filled the room. Emily and Tom had stayed up all night to finish the decorations. It was so beautiful that Bessie could only stand and stare at it. Then Auntie and Uncle Tom showed her the present hidden among the branches that was just for her. And every day for the next month, they managed to find another present on the tree for her.

Bessie quickly grew to love the Willifords. And she adored the big, white house with the wide front porch on Tugalo Street that had become her home. She had never known such luxury; every room had its own fireplace. Toccoa was a much bigger and busier town than Carnesville. Sometimes she could hear the trains rolling into town, whistles blowing, and there seemed to always be activity on the streets. She still missed her siblings, but Auntie and Uncle Tom were more than willing to take her to visit her sisters Lucy and Lettie May whenever she wanted.

A couple of months after coming to live in Toccoa, Bessie attended her first Missionary Society meeting. Auntie Emily was an active member of the group and, on this day, it was her turn to host the meeting in her home. The ladies, in hats and gloves and on their best behavior, sat in a circle of chairs in the parlor. Auntie put four-year-old Bessie on the chair beside her. Then, going around the circle, each lady introduced herself by saying her name and adding "I'm a Baptist." Auntie spoke right up when it was her turn. "I'm Emily Williford and I'm a Baptist."

Finally all eyes turned to Bessie, sitting very still, hands in her lap. She looked around the circle, took a deep breath and spoke. "I'm Bessie Ayers and I guess I'm a Baptist, too." With that, her life as a Methodist was left behind.

THREE

A NEW FAMILY AND A NEW LIFE

By the end of her first year with the Willifords, young Bessie Ayers had happily settled in with her new family. Her foster parents were so pleased with her that they decided to bring a second child into their home. They contacted the Ayers cousins once again and, in a short time, Bessie's younger sister Lettie May joined the Williford household. Bessie was bursting with excitement when her sister came to live in Toccoa, but the first time she saw May-May climb onto Uncle Tom's lap, she almost hated her. It was hard to accept the fact that she was going to have to share all the love and attention that had belonged to her alone. But her jealously was short-lived, crowded out by her love for May-May and the joy of once more having a sister around. The deep bond forged between these two would deepen and endure throughout their lives.

In 1905, the girls' eldest brother, Jeremiah, died of tuberculosis. It was just one more sadness for the Ayers family to endure. Bessie and May-May tried to visit their siblings even more often after that and their older sister Lucy became a frequent visitor to the big house in Toccoa.

Emily Williford was a businesswoman in a time when few women ventured outside their homes for professional reasons. Tall and substantially built, she was an impressive person. The milliner's shop she owned in downtown Toccoa sold hats to most of the ladies in town. Bessie and May-May spent countless hours in the shop, playing with brightly colored scraps of velvet and lace, watching Mrs. Williford construct her creations and listening to the exchanges between Auntie and her customers. Bessie was particularly interested in her foster mother's collection techniques. While some paid cash for their purchases, many customers ask her to charge their fine hats.

"That's fine," Mrs. Williford would tell them. "I'll be around to collect."

And she was as good as her word. In those days bills were not mailed to customers. Mrs. Williford would leave her shop several times a month and go to the homes of those women who owed her money. There she would pleasantly, but firmly ask for payment. Sometimes she would allow Bessie to accompany her on these visits. Bessie admired Auntie and believed her to be fearless. She wanted to be just like her. When she was older, Auntie sometimes let Bessie make some of the collections on her own.

Bessie was only fourteen years old when she met the man who would be her husband. She first saw T. Orr Fisher on a Sunday morning at the First Baptist Church in Toccoa. He noticed her the same day and made sure he was introduced to her after the service. No one was surprised that he was attracted to the pretty, petite girl with the big, brown eyes. And the attraction was mutual. He was a handsome, smiling young man. The son of a shopkeeper in nearby Lavonia, his first job had been with the railroad, but the work didn't suit him. He had changed professions soon after that and now, because of the dashing nature of his job, he was the talk of the young ladies in Toccoa. He sold Reo automobiles!

In the infancy of that business, there were few local dealerships, certainly none in North Georgia, but Orr Fisher was an enterprising young man. He would travel by train to the closest Reo dealership, usually several states away, and purchase one car. Then he'd drive the new vehicle back to Georgia and go from town to town until he found a buyer. Once the sale was complete, he'd repeat the process

It was not an easy way to make a living, but he loved motor cars and the job brought him a certain amount of fame. People ran out of their houses to the edge of the street when they heard Orr Fisher and one of his automobiles approaching. Some marveled at this wonderful invention and a few cursed it, declaring it scared the horses and other livestock, but Orr enjoyed every minute. He knew he was riding the wave of the future.

For the first years of their courtship, Bessie and Orr saw each other only at church functions or when the young man visited her in her home. Their meetings were always under the watchful eyes of the Willifords. But by the time she was sixteen, Bessie was slipping away for afternoon rides with him. Friends, including May-May, who was a more than willing conspirator, usually accompanied them on these rides. Most of the outings were short jaunts around the countryside, but occasionally they ventured further afield. One favorite activity was packing a picnic lunch and driving to nearby Toccoa Falls, where they ate their sandwiches beside the rushing water.

Bessie and Orr married in the Toccoa First Baptist Church on November 26, 1913, and moved into the house on Tugalo Street with Thomas and Emily Williford. With Orr on the road so often selling his cars, it was a most reasonable arrangement for the newlyweds. It was especially convenient when Bessie became pregnant. Having another child in the house was an exciting prospect for the Willifords and they were pleased to be able to pamper and care for Bessie.

In May of 1914, Lettie May Ayers turned twenty-one. At that time, when the youngest of the surviving Ayers children reached legal majority, the inheritance from their parents could be divided among them. Their uncle Sanford Ayers was willing to purchase the land he'd farmed for so many years. Only Lucy, the eldest daughter, chose to take her share in land. The others sold their portions to their uncle. Bessie and Orr did not even have to discuss what they would do with her share. They were frugal people by nature and simply put the money away for the future.

The birth of Emily Elizabeth Fisher on October 4, 1914, shook up the quiet of the Williford household. Named for Bessie's foster mother, the tiny girl became the center of the family's attention. From the first day, she was showered with affection.

Orr's father, Levi Fisher, died in February of the next year, but not before seeing the newest Fisher family member and holding the baby in his arms. After his death, his widow Masena continued to run the big store in Lavonia. Orr and Bessie often drove to the nearby town so that Emily could spend time with her grandmother. As Emily grew older, her father entertained her with stories of his childhood. When he was about four years old, he told her, he began spending time at the family store. It seemed to be a huge place to the little boy, but he loved being there. There was always something going on and people came in the store all day long. He especially loved helping out when his mother would allow him to locate the different spools of thread requested by her customers.

Orr still spent much of his time traveling, working hard to build up his business. He would set off in a newly acquired vehicle with only the vaguest of ideas about routes and destinations. The dirt roads he drove had not been constructed with automobiles in mind. Getting stuck in the mud was as common as having a tire hang up on a deep rut. He forded streams, slept in his car when no lodging was available and was often lost. Road maps were still far in the future. While Orr was certainly a pioneer in auto sales, he wasn't the only one. When two salesmen visited the same town at the same time, tempers could flare. It rarely came to blows, but harsh words were often exchanged.

Mammy and Daddy Tom, as young Emily took to calling the Willifords, were the first people in Toccoa to have indoor plumbing. Mrs. Williford hired a plumber who had recently moved there from Sweden to build her a bathroom. When he'd finished, it was a tile and chrome work of art. She was inordinately proud of it and kept the room spotless and gleaming.

Emily Fisher was a happy child who made friends easily and the Williford house was one of the favorite gathering places for the neighborhood children. At three years old, not only was she a charming friend, but she possessed a lot of toys and willingly shared them. Another attraction at the Williford house was the children's playhouse, fashioned from an old piano crate, in the backyard.

The new bathroom caused quite a sensation. Almost every child who came to the house made some excuse to visit it. It wasn't long before Mrs. Williford complained to Bessie that all those children were making a mess of the place, splashing water all over and leaving towels on the floor. Bessie had a serious talk with her daughter.

"Emily, your friends are making a mess in Mammy's bathroom. You must tell them, when they want to go to the bathroom, that they must go home."

"But if they go home, they won't come back," Emily worried.

"Oh, of course, they will."

Emily wasn't so sure they would, but knew arguing would do no good.

Several days later, Bessie was in the backyard when she became aware of a foul odor. She looked around the yard, but could find no cause for it. Finally she opened the little door to the playhouse and the smell immediately intensified. There on the floor was a chamber pot, which showed signs of recent use, and a roll of toilet paper. Emily had set up her own bathroom to keep her friends from leaving. From then on, Emily's friends were welcome in the Willifords' indoor facilities.

Emily's parents and the Willifords indulged her. When her father traveled, he always took along an empty suitcase. It was in that case that he would put all the presents he bought for his daughter on his travels. At Christmas time, she received so many gifts that her mother decided it wouldn't be right to give them all to one child at one time. Those that were deemed to be excessive were stored in the top of an old, unused icebox at the end of the hall. From there they would be doled one at a time over the next few months when Emily's behavior merited a reward.

FOUR

A MOVE TO ATLANTA

Orr Fisher became quite well known as a car salesman. In 1917, his cousin, F.E. Maffett, offered him a job. Maffett owned a Dodge dealership in Atlanta. It was too good an opportunity to miss. Orr moved his little family to Atlanta and went to work selling cars on West Peachtree Street, while Bessie set up housekeeping in an upstairs apartment in Inman Park.

Atlanta experienced a devastating fire the year the Fishers came to town. It began off Decatur Street, well southeast of where the Fishers lived, and swept north and east, destroying businesses and ravaging residential neighborhoods along North Avenue and Boulevard. The Army was dispatched and used dynamite on some streets to try and create a firebreak. Fire companies from surrounding cities dispatched their pumper trucks to Atlanta. The blaze was finally brought under control late the same night.

There were no fatalities, but thousands were left homeless and many people, with nowhere else to go, spent more than one night in Piedmont Park. The Fishers' home was never in danger, but no one in the city escaped the smoke and soot. Most people, at least those who could, stayed in their homes with the doors and windows shut tight. As it had before, the city set about rebuilding almost as soon as the fire was out.

Orr Fisher had an appreciation for owning land. He and Bessie had often talked about it. "Invest in something you can put your feet on," he'd said many times. In 1919, the young couple made their first real estate purchase. They looked around and found what they believed was a good piece of property in nearby Dekalb County. Before making any decision, they had Tom Williford come down from Toccoa and walk the land with them. He approved of their choice and, using the money she'd inherited from her parents, Bessie purchased the 150-acre farm from William Bradbury. The land, complete with a farmhouse and out buildings, had been owned by a succession of families over the past century. At the time of purchase, Bradbury had rented it out and Orr quickly worked out an arrangement with the family who was living there. They would work the farm and he would take a percentage of what they made from their crops as rent.

When Emily was five years old, they moved from their apartment to a house on Fifth Street. Their home soon became the center of activity for their extended families. Lucy Ayers, Bessie's older sister, had studied at the Georgia Southern College for Women and taught school in Carnesville. But when the Fishers moved there, she and a teacher friend got jobs in Atlanta and took a room in their home. Atlanta was a very fast-paced, cosmopolitan place to live for two young women from north Georgia.

Bessie's brother Ernest was also a frequent visitor. Emily adored her uncle and found his antics greatly amusing. One cold winter evening, Bessie, Orr, Ernest and Emily left the dinner table and gathered around the fireplace in the parlor. The good food and the warmth of the fire combined to make Orr drowsy. In minutes, he'd nodded off, his chin dropping almost to his chest. Ernest's eyes lit with mischief. He left his chair and, using soot from the edge of the fireplace, painted a beard, mustache and heavy eyebrows on Orr's face. Ernest's touch was so deft and light that the sleeping man never stirred. Bessie and Emily could barely stifle their merriment. It burst forth when Orr opened his eyes. Amid shouts of laughter, they encouraged him to go look in the mirror.

Although he tried to pretend to be angry, Orr had to laugh along with the others when he saw his newly decorated face.

Bessie's cousin, Belton Bond spent three months in the Fisher home. He had been elected to the Georgia General Assembly as a representative of Franklin County. He was, however, still a very young man. Before his mother would allow him to spend three months away from home in the dangerous city of Atlanta, she extracted his promise that, during that time, he would live with Orr and Bessie.

Emily's education got off to a rocky start. At six years old, she was enrolled in the first grade at the 10th Street School, but she had no intention of going. When the time came for her to leave the house on the first day of school, the little girl hid under her bed and refused to come out. Cajoling and persuading did no good. Orr even threatened her with a whipping. She volunteered to take the spanking if they'd just let her stay home. Finally they had to pull her from her hiding place and force her out of the house. Bessie went to school with her daughter that first day and the next few days. She'd sit quietly at the back of the room until the activities of the class were well underway. Then she'd slip out. Emily participated happily with her classmates until she realized her mother had gone. Then there would be a storm of tears and schoolwork would cease until she had been comforted and the tears dried.

Her aversion to education was short-lived and school soon became a favorite place for the little girl. She was an excellent student and popular with the other children. Every morning she would leave home and confidently make the short walk to school. Every afternoon she'd make the reverse trip home where her mother would be waiting with an afternoon snack, ready to hear all about the day.

Bessie and Orr were people of modest means who would rather save than spend money, but they would splurge on items for their precious daughter. Bessie could rarely resist a bit of finery in which to dress her Emily. She once paid $25, a staggering sum in those days, for a hat because she loved the way Emily looked in that frilly creation. One morning when May-May was visiting them, the two sisters debated a downtown shopping trip. May-May was hesitant. She glanced at their plain clothes and said, "Oh, Bessie, we don't look good enough to go downtown."

Bessie just laughed. "We'll just put the hat on Emily and stand behind her. No one will pay any attention to us."

Orr gave Emily a Victrola and a complete set of Enrico Caruso's records. The child was thrilled. She spent hours on end playing the records and listening to the soaring voice of the famous tenor. As the months and years passed, more and more records of all types were added to her collection. In 1922, WSB, the first commercial radio station in Georgia, began broadcasting from Atlanta. Soon the radio became a fixture in the Fisher household and the family gathered around it every evening after dinner.

The family moved to a large upstairs apartment on Spring Street so that Orr would be nearer to his West Peachtree Street office. During the early 1920's, the automobile industry grew at a frantic pace and F.E. Maffett, Inc., grew right along with it. Orr Fisher was now sales manager. Cars were no longer novelties. They were fast becoming the country's favorite mode of transportation and a number of dealerships dotted West Peachtree Street. There was so much interest in automobiles that *The Atlanta Constitution* ran a regular feature called "Hobbies of Automobile Men." In 1925, T.O. Fisher, or "Take Order" Fisher as he'd come to be called in the business, was featured. His photo, embellished by a drawing that showed him holding a pitchfork and decked out as a farmer, headed the small write up. His hobby, it was reported, was farming.

Fisher loved the Dekalb County farm and the whole family spent time there. A drive to the farm was a frequent Sunday after-noon diversion. It could also be an adventure. Once Orr turned the car off of Ponce de Leon Avenue, there was no more paving. They'd bounce along the dirt track that was Briarcliff Road for eight or ten miles, sometimes having to stop so Orr could change a damaged tire. The trip to the farm always took several hours.

Emily looked forward to these visits. There were so many children there that she never lacked for playmates and sometimes her parents let her bring along a friend from town. The farm offered wide-open spaces for running around and playing games. There were dogs and cats in abundance, along with other animals the city children rarely saw. Emily especially loved the sawdust pile. Climbing to the top was the most exciting thing she knew.

When the weather was bad, Emily stayed in the farmhouse while Bessie visited with the farmer's wife. Orr and the farmer made their usual check of the property. One cold, blustery day, the women sat near the fire in the parlor. Emily squeezed next to her mother on the sofa and the farmer's wife sat in a rocker with a toddler—a girl of about three—at her knee. While the women chatted, Emily watched the little girl fuss and pull at her mother's skirt. The woman would push her away, but the child kept coming back.

The child's distress grew and finally Bessie asked, "What's wrong? What does she want?"

"Oh, she's just pestering me for a dip of snuff, but I'm not going to give it to her now." She pushed the child away again.

"You don't give her *snuff*?" Bessie asked, horrified.

"Well, just a little—every once in a while," the woman said, silently shifting the tobacco in her own cheek. "But she's gotten used to it now and she sure does like it."

§๑

Bessie's younger sister May-May married Harry Noell and they had a daughter whom they named Harriett. Nearly the same age,

Harriett and Emily became very close. They were more like sisters than cousins. Emily was saddened when Harry and May-May moved to North Carolina, but the families still got together at the Willifords' Toccoa home every Christmas. And once a year, they would visit Granny Fisher in Lavonia where Emily was able to see and play with her many Fisher cousins.

In 1924, a new cousin came into Emily's life. Helen Pittman, daughter of Norman and Lucy Pittman, had been born in China. She was the same age as Emily and, the year she turned ten, her father died. The family left China and returned to the United States and settled in Atlanta near the Fishers. Emily thought her cousin was quite an exotic creature. Tall, with long, shining black hair, she spoke fluent Chinese, French, and perfect English. In fact, her English was so perfect that Emily sometimes had trouble understanding it.

Helen fascinated her American cousin with stories of far away lands and unusual people. She had seen and done things Emily never even knew existed. But Helen, whose education to this point had been in the hands of private tutors, was completely out of her element in a public school. Emily took charge. She walked Helen to school and showed her where to put her coat, where to sit and what books she needed. She taught her about the daily schedule and introduced her to the other children. Emily was amazed to learn that Helen knew nothing of modern music or picture shows or popular books. So she helped with her cultural education as well.

Helen's mother had been accustomed to elaborate entertaining and she continued that practice after arriving in Atlanta. Every Thursday afternoon she held open house. The ladies who attended were treated to sparkling conversation, the latest fashion news and delectable refreshments provided by the city's best caterer. The leftovers from these events provided young Helen with very special lunches every Friday. When she unpacked her collection of delicious tidbits, the other children would gather around to see what she'd brought. Soon they were all asking for a taste of this or a bite of that. Polite and not wanting to disappoint any of her new friends, Helen would share her lunch. Soon she would have given it all away and she'd go to Emily and tell her. Emily would then have to share her own lunch with her overly generous cousin. This would have to stop, Emily realized, or neither she nor Helen would ever have a full lunch on Friday. So she went to the other children, one by one, and explained the situation.

"Okay," she told them, "when she gives you something, you must give her something in return. Otherwise Helen will have no lunch."

The tactic worked and, after that, Helen always had plenty of food for lunch.

The Fishers prospered in Atlanta. They were comfortable with the life they had made for themselves and well respected by the community. But Orr realized that, as sales manager, he had risen as far as he was likely to at Maffett Motor Company. So when he had a chance to open his own Dodge dealership in the west Georgia town of LaGrange, he didn't hesitate.

FIVE

LIFE IN LAGRANGE

In 1926, much of life in LaGrange, Georgia, centered around the huge Callaway Textile Mills. The company was the town's main employer and contributed in many ways to the health, social and cultural life of the community. It was a pretty little town surrounded by miles and miles of fertile farmland and Orr Fisher thought it was the perfect place to open his own automobile business.

The Fishers moved first into a small house on Ben Hill Avenue and Orr established his Dodge Brothers Motor Vehicles dealership at 109 Greenville Street. He was completely preoccupied with getting his business up and running and gave little thought to his surroundings, but Bessie and Emily were less than happy with the move. Their friends, family and familiar surroundings had been left behind them in Atlanta. They found themselves in a strange town among people they didn't know. It was late autumn and the school year was already in session, but Bessie was so lonely that she kept Emily home for the first week just for the company.

After a few days of this isolation, Emily grew restive. One afternoon she announced she was going to find some friends.

"Now how are you going to do that?" her mother asked with a smile.

Emily had no doubt about that. "I'll just walk up the street and knock on doors and say 'I'm Emily Elizabeth. Do you have any children?' And then they'll come out and I'll smile at them and they'll smile at me and come to my house and play."

Emily did exactly that and the results nearly overwhelmed her mother. In an hour, almost 20 children showed up at the Fisher house. They romped with Emily in the yard and played in her room, while Bessie wondered what in the world she could give them as a snack. She finally baked some cookies and served them with glasses of milk. The next day, Emily started school in LaGrange.

In spite of her initial misgivings, Bessie found it as easy to make friends as her daughter did. The family joined the First Baptist Church and the Highland Country Club. Bessie became active in the Missionary Society and the Women's Club and Orr became a member of the Rotary Club. On a biographical form he completed for the service organization, he wrote that his favorite song was *Sing Me to Sleep*, his favorite food was fried chicken and his hobby was motoring.

After a few years, the family purchased a big brick home on North Greenwood Street. Although they were solidly settled in LaGrange, Orr and Bessie held onto their Dekalb County farm.

It was during this time that Orr Fisher stopped selling Dodge automobiles and began marketing Oldsmobiles. Only the manufacturers changed. He continued doing business from the same location and, for the most part, kept the same customers.

Emily Fisher was a happy child and she thrived in LaGrange. By the time she reached high school, the outgoing, bubbly young woman had a throng of friends and was considered an excellent student. She enjoyed school and sports and was a member of the Cotillion Club. Her parents celebrated her sixteenth birthday by giving her a little green roadster automobile, complete with a rumble seat.

She loved driving as much as her father did and took that little car all over the countryside, usually with several friends in tow. She would use any excuse to get behind the wheel. In fact, she often helped out a young friend who had a paper route. When Emily showed up, he could ditch his bicycle and ride around in style, tossing papers from her little car.

While she enjoyed school, studying did not fill all of Emily's time. She and her friends spent the long summer days playing tennis and swimming at the country club and there were dances and parties year round. The Cotillion Club sponsored big dances twice a year, usually with a theme. One year, the boys were required to pay admission to the dance according to how much their dates weighed. The going rate was a penny a pound. Although Emily was always in demand as a date, that particular theme might have made her especially popular with the young men. When she weighed in at the door, her pleased date had to pay only 92 cents for their admission.

The Fishers often entertained friends and relatives from Atlanta and north Georgia. One of Emily's favorites was her cousin Helen Pittman. When Helen came, there seemed to be one party after another. They especially enjoyed the prom parties. These events were held at private homes and the boys and girls arrived separately. A dessert table was set up with a large selection of treats and each girl was given a paper prom card. The prom cards were similar to dance cards, but with spaces for about 10 promenades. While the refreshments were sampled, the boys went to the girls and signed up for the individual proms. Once the cards were filled, a bell rang, signaling the beginning of the first prom. The girls found the boys who were first on their cards and the couples left the house. They strolled slowly up the quiet residential lane, taking the opportunity to talk together and, maybe, steal a kiss or two outside the watchful eyes of the adult chaperons. After about ten minutes, the bell rang again and the first prom was over. The guests returned to the house where they changed partners and waited for the next bell.

Emily was an exceptional student and skipped half a grade in high school. As a result, she finished her senior year at LaGrange High School in December of 1931. For the next six months, she attended Bible and business classes at LaGrange College.

While she liked the people at the college, Emily's dreams reached far beyond her hometown. She wanted to attend Emerson College in Boston, but her parents wouldn't even consider allowing their seventeen-year-old daughter to travel that far from home. In the fall of 1932, they reached a compromise and Emily left for Shorter College in Rome, Georgia. It turned out to be a less than satisfying experience for both her and the college.

One of the first things she discovered at Shorter was that she was expected to take Biology. Emily wanted no part of anything that involved dissecting frogs and was ready to leave the school right then, but she'd never been a quitter. She stuck it out, hating every minute of the class. Studying French was another trial. Try as she might, she couldn't read it, speak it, or understand it. The only good thing about the course was the friendship she developed with her instructor's daughter. She always wondered if that friendship accounted for his kindness at the end of the year when he called her in for a conference.

"Are you ever going to take French again?" he asked.

"Never!" she declared with certainty.

He nodded. "Then I'll pass you—on the condition that you never tell anyone that I was your French teacher."

Emily chose to spend her two final years of college at the University of Georgia in Athens. Helen Pittman was attending the university at the same time and the two cousins roomed together.

One weekend during her first year at the University, Emily went home with Helen to Atlanta. They were surprised to find a young man staying at the house. He had come from China where his parents were missionaries and this was his first trip to the United States. Helen's mother had graciously opened her home to him. The girls found him to be a pleasant companion and the three young people passed the time playing games, listening to music and playing cards. A few days after they returned to school, Helen's mother called to tell them that the young man from China had fallen ill with typhoid.

Except to be sorry for him, Emily gave the young man's sickness no more thought until a week or so later when Helen began to complain that she wasn't feeling well. Emily was not concerned. Helen had always been a bit fragile and always seemed to be complaining of one ailment or another. This time, however, it appeared to be more than a minor complaint.

"I'm really sick," she told Emily. "I have to go home. I'm scared."

Helen had already spent her allowance for the month, so Emily lent her the money for a train ticket home. The room seemed very lonely after Helen had gone. Emily invited a friend from down the hall to come and sleep in Helen's bed.

Helen's mother met her at the station with an ambulance. A short time later, the emergency room doctor diagnosed her as having typhoid. When news of Helen's illness reached the University, the administration acted quickly. Emily and the girl who'd been unlucky enough to spend a night in Helen's bed were immediately quarantined. They were locked in a room in the campus infirmary and allowed no face-to-face contact with anyone else. Their meals were brought on trays. The door was unlocked and trays shoved inside. Then the door was locked again.

Emily was furious. She felt fine. If she were going to contract the disease, she reasoned, she would already be sick—like Helen was. She was not afraid of getting typhoid, but she was very unhappy at being held prisoner. And she was not about to accept such treatment without a fight. Besides, she had a date Friday night and had no intention of canceling it. Late Friday afternoon, she slipped out an infirmary window and made her way across campus to her dorm. She found the door to her room had been padlocked, but that barely slowed her down. Using another student's room for access, she climbed out on the roof and crossed to the window of her own room. She went inside, got into an evening dress and telephoned her date. After arranging to meet him away from the dormitory, she retraced her route across the roof and was off for a night out. After that, the administration more or less gave up on the idea of quarantine.

℘

In March of 1934, Emily Williford—Emily Fisher's beloved Mammy—died. Daddy Tom had her buried beside her first husband and reserved the plot on her other side for himself. Her death was a terrible blow to him. She'd been his close companion, his best friend for so many years that her absence was terrible for him to endure. After only a short time, he left his home in Toccoa and went to live with Bessie and Orr. His health was poor and Bessie gave up most of her outside activities to stay home and care for him.

When Emily came home that summer, she found life was very different with Daddy Tom around. Bessie stayed busy caring for him. She made special meals for him and tried to find things that would interest him. The family had to be extra quiet because he seemed to nap all the time. One afternoon the old man was sitting on the porch taking the sun. Bessie suggested that Emily go out and talk with him. Emily went, but was back in only a few seconds.

"I think something is wrong with him," she told her mother. "He just keeps rocking and talking to himself."

Fearful that his condition had worsened, Bessie hurried outside where her foster father was placidly rocking.

"Are you all right, Uncle Tom? Emily said you were talking to yourself."

A gentle smile crossed his face. "I'm fine, Bessie. I was just talking with my memories."

Emily felt tears in her eyes. She was happy for Daddy Tom and realized it was a great blessing that he had his memories to talk with. When he died a year later, he was laid to rest beside his cherished wife.

Six

When Emily Met Remer

Emily joined the Kappa Delta sorority at the University and, during her senior year, decided to move into the sorority house. She was surprised to discover just how crowded the house was. Each of the rooms, designed for two girls, was furnished with a bureau and a double bed. Not only was she expected to share a room, but a bed as well. This was unwelcome news for an only child. She hated the idea of having to sleep in a bed with another girl.

Once her room in the Kappa Delta house was assigned, Emily made a telephone call. Later that day, her parents delivered a twin bed to her. They moved it into her room, right across from the double bed that was already there. Emily was quite possessive about her little bed. On busy nights when there was a football game or a big dance, she put a sign on it that read: "There better not be anybody in this bed when I come home". When she returned to the house after an evening out, there were often three or four girls lined up like firewood in the double bed, but she never found anyone sleeping in hers.

Her parents stayed very busy while Emily was away at school. Orr's business was brisk and Bessie had made quite a reputation for herself as a gardener. In the early spring of 1935, the *LaGrange Daily News* featured her in an article about creating and maintaining a rock garden. Her rock garden was described as "one of the loveliest in the city." Bessie believed that ugly or unsightly areas of a yard could be transformed into lovely, lush garden spots by the use of ponds, waterfalls and rock gardens, and the reporter passed this advice on to his readers.

Emily Fisher had always had a flair for dramatics. She loved performing and had no fear of audiences. After graduating from the University of Georgia in 1935, she applied to and was accepted by the American Academy of Dramatic Arts. That fall, Bessie and Orr took their daughter to New York City and got her settled in the American Women's Club—a very respectable residential hotel for women. One of Emily's college roommates, Louisa Stephens, accompanied them on the trip.

The four Georgians had a wonderful time in the big city. They went sightseeing. They dined out and shopped. When the time came for her friend and parents to return home, Emily begged Louisa to stay on for a while.

"Well, maybe I could, for a few days anyway," Louisa said, allowing herself to be persuaded. "My parents gave me $100 before I came."

Emily assured her that such a huge amount of money would last a long time and Louisa moved her bags into Emily's room at the Women's Club. It was a heady time for two girls from Georgia. Louisa's visit turned into something more permanent. She quickly found a job at the cosmetic counter at Bergdorf-Goodman and Emily began her classes at Carnegie Hall. They loved what they were doing, but soon discovered that New York was a very expensive city in which to live. As the days passed, it became apparent that their money was not going to stretch very far. They hated the idea of having to economize even more and decided their wisest action would be to find a cheaper place to live. They rented a small, second floor walk-up in a shabby neighborhood out near the Columbia University campus. To make their money go even further, they invited two other girls to move in with them.

Because of her association with the Academy, Emily was able to see most performances at Carnegie Hall and other theaters for free, but she couldn't always arrange the same for her friends. More often than not, she went to the shows alone, then caught the elevated and changed to the subway to travel home. A sprawling city park lay near their apartment and Emily often left the subway and cut through the green space on her way home. The short cut reduced her walk by more than five minutes. She had never been a fearful girl and living in New York hadn't changed her. Even having her fur coat stolen had not robbed her of her natural optimism and trust.

One night after midnight, Emily was walking briskly along the paved path through the park when she thought she heard footsteps. She listened harder. Yes, they were definitely footsteps and they seemed to be matching her own, stride for stride. She sped up. So did the walker behind her. She walked even faster. For once, Emily was frightened. She was nearly running by the time she reached the end of the park, but there was still a spark of defiance in her. She spun around on the sidewalk to confront her pursuer and came face to face with an uniformed police officer.

"Oh," she said in relief, "you about scared me to death."

His stern expression didn't waver. "Where are you going, young lady?"

"To my apartment. It's right down here." She gestured toward the end of the block.

"All right. I'll watch you. And don't you *ever* come through this park alone at night again. Now go on and get in your apartment!"

She meekly obeyed and never again walked through the park at night.

Emily's freedom was short-lived. When her parents arrived for a Christmas visit, they were horrified to learn where their only child was living. No amount of protest on Emily's part could change their minds. Before they left town, she had been returned to the safe harbor of the American Women's Club.

The work at the Academy was hard, but Emily didn't mind hard work. She appeared in a number of plays and, while she enjoyed them all, the comedies were her favorites. She loved making people laugh. What she did not enjoy was the dictatorial attitude displayed by some of the directors. She especially did not appreciate being yelled at.

Still, she could have tolerated the directors' rudeness in order to achieve her goal of becoming an actress, but Emily gradually became aware of something else that would stand between her and a successful career. She simply wasn't pushy enough. She had to admit to herself that she'd never be the sort of person who could put her foot in a door and hold it there, demanding she be hired. She could not imagine being happy with the years of rejection she knew would be waiting for anyone trying to make it on the stage. So when the school year ended, she packed up and returned to Georgia.

Back at home, it was easy to pick up her old life, visiting with friends, going to parties and swimming at the club. It was a very pleasant existence and she might have settled right into it had it not been for her parents. Orr and Bessie had never lived lives of leisure and they weren't going to have their daughter doing so. They told her she would have to get a job.

Emily had never given working much thought, but she applied to the telephone company in Atlanta and the local school system. The teaching job came through first. They called her for an interview and she nearly lost the job before she ever got it. Her age and appearance worked against her. The middle-aged man who met with her was concerned that so young and slight a woman would not be able to control a class of ten-year-olds.

"Just let me try," she said. "I think I can do it. If not, I'll quit."

She won him over and got the job.

In the fall of 1937, she began teaching fifth grade at Rosemont School, in a little community of the same name, a few miles outside of LaGrange. It was a sobering experience for a young woman accustomed to the stately halls of the University and, before that, the orderly classrooms of LaGrange High School. Rosemont School was a primitive, one-story wooden building. All of the classrooms opened directly to the outside. There was no indoor plumbing and the wood stoves in each classroom supplied the only heat.

On her first day, Emily found herself facing a classroom full of 40 fidgety, inattentive students. Even though she was in mid-sentence when the recess bell rang, the children all got to their feet and began talking and moving toward the door. Emily knew she could not begin her teaching career by letting the children call the shots. She moved fast and got to the door ahead of them where she planted her petite, 5'3" frame solidly in the middle of the doorway, arms crossed over her chest. The students stopped in their tracks, puzzled by her behavior. They stared at her uncertainly and she stared back. Then it began to sink in that she was not going to allow them to leave. They shifted from foot to foot, then finally returned to their desks. When everyone was seated, Emily told them how they were expected to leave the room—in an orderly manner after she had released them. She then dismissed them for recess and they quietly filed out of the room.

In spite of the rocky start, Emily discovered that her students were bright and eager to learn. But they were hampered by a lack of supplies. The school was too poor to even have a library. Emily began bringing in her own books from home for the students to use. By the end of the first month, her class boasted its own library at the back of the room.

The children were, for the most part, as poor as their school. One morning Emily asked one of them what he'd had for breakfast and the little boy answered that he'd had turnip greens. As the conversation grew to include the rest of the class, Emily realized that the children she taught were lucky to have food of any kind before coming to school. From that day on, she managed to create a reason at least once a week for a "party" so that she could bring as much food as she could manage for the children in her care.

§◦

The Fisher family's next door neighbors on North Greenwood Street were the Finchers. Mr. Fincher traveled and, in order to have a male presence in the house, Mrs. Fincher converted her big basement into three rooms for young men boarders. Two of the boarders in 1938 were Remer Crum and Russell Redding. The three Fincher daughters, Mildred, Miriam and Phyllis, were particularly taken with Remer. Tall and handsome, with a slow smile and a quick wit, he was the most dashing young man they'd ever met. Mildred, who was finishing her junior year of high school, knew he was too old for her, but she thought he would be perfect for her next door neighbor, Emily Fisher. Recently returned from New York, Emily seemed to represent the height of sophistication and chic. Mildred took it upon herself to bring these two special people together.

"You just have to meet him," she told Emily. "He's smart and good looking and, oh, he'd be just right for you."

Emily smiled, but wasn't particularly interested. She was already seeing a young man on a fairly regular basis and wasn't anxious to meet anyone else. But Mildred kept after her. Finally one Saturday afternoon Emily gave in.

"Who was that?" her mother asked when Emily hung up the phone.

"It was Mildred. She wants me to ride to the post office with her and this young man next door."

"Well, I don't believe I'd go," Bessie said doubtfully.

Emily shrugged. She was grading papers and didn't mind taking a break. "I don't have anything else to do."

§D

David Alpheus Remer Crum was born in Homerville, Georgia, in 1868, and his family moved to Savannah when he was only five years old. He attended the University of Georgia for two quarters, then returned home to Savannah. There he studied law, or read the law as it was called, with a small legal firm. Shortly after the turn of the century, he moved to the small south Georgia farming town of Vienna and opened a law practice with J.G. James.

During a business trip to the nearby town of Hawkinsville, he met Florence Hamilton. A recent graduate of Wesleyan College, she was a beautiful, elegant young woman from a prominent family of farmers and bankers. He was taken with her from the first minute he saw her and courted her very determinedly. The two were married within the year.

They set up housekeeping in Vienna, but within a few years moved to a big, rambling house on West 14th Avenue in Cordele. David Crum opened a law office on 7th Avenue, the town's wide main street, and they joined the First Methodist Church. The big house was necessary for theirs was a large family. Five daughters—Sara, Mary, Florence, Malette and Lily—and two sons—Remer and Charles—easily filled the house. In fact, within a few years David Crum built an addition to the house. He always said it was to accommodate his eldest daughters' clothes. Remer Hamilton Crum, born February 11, 1913, was the couple's fifth child and the first son.

Florence was a loving wife and mother and an active church and club woman, but in 1923 she was stricken with Parkinson's disease. David was frantic. He tried everything he could to help her, taking her to any doctor in the country who might hold out hope, but it was no use. She grew steadily worse until her activities were sadly restricted and she was confined to bed most of the time. Her husband and children cared for her and did their best to keep her happy and comfortable.

Charles Crum idolized his older brother and followed him everywhere. Remer was an accomplished athlete and his brother wanted to be just like him. In the summer, they roamed the farms and fields around Cordele. One hot day, they were playing in an old barn on an abandoned farm when Charles fell through the rotting wood of the loft and broke his toe. He knew he'd never be able to walk the miles back to their house. Remer didn't give it a thought. Without a complaint, he hoisted his little brother onto his back and carried him all the way home.

David's law practice did well and he was a respected member of the community. He was elected to the Georgia State Senate and, in 1925, he was appointed judge of the Crisp County Superior Court. He was also one of the driving forces behind the Crisp County Power Project which would eventually harness the Flint River to provide water and electricity to the entire area. The power project became the only county-owned and operated hydroelectric plant in the nation.

Remer and his siblings all attended Cordele High School. Remer maintained his grades well enough, but the area in which he really excelled was athletics. He was a member of the varsity baseball and football teams his junior and senior years. He was also an avid fisherman and hunter. Remer graduated from high school in 1929, only three months before the sudden death of his father.

David Crum had left his courthouse office early on Friday afternoon, September 6th, complaining of feeling vaguely unwell. At 5:30 that afternoon, he died at his home of a stroke, shocking his family and the community. Judge Crum had been well loved and greatly respected. In a lengthy write up, the *Cordele Dispatch* called him "an indulgent and kindly father, devoted husband, loyal citizen and conscientious and scholarly lawyer and jurist." Although he could be a stern man, he was known to always look out for the less fortunate people who came before his bench. The whole county mourned his loss.

With his father gone and his mother in poor health, Remer wasn't sure he should leave Cordele to attend college, but his mother insisted that he go. The young man had been planning to attend the Georgia Institute of Technology, but hadn't yet been accepted. At Florence's urging, he telephoned the school and managed to work things out. In late September he headed north to Atlanta to begin his engineering studies. The second year of his education was spent at Middle Georgia College in Cochran and his final year at South Georgia College in Tifton. After school, Remer went to work with the Soil Conservation Department. His job took him all over the state.

In 1935, Florence Crum passed away. Young Remer found himself very much alone in the world. He concentrated more and more on his work. In 1937, the state sent him to LaGrange, Georgia, where he found a room in the basement of the Fincher home on North Greenwood Street.

<p>

He had been in town only a week or so when Mildred Fincher told him she wanted him to meet Emily Fisher. On Saturday afternoon, he was going to drive downtown to the post office to mail a letter and invited Mildred to come along. She suggested that Emily go with them. She and Remer got in his car and drove up into the drive of the house next door. Emily Fisher came out of her front door and Remer couldn't help but notice she was a very pretty young woman. She wore what Mildred considered to be a very stylish New York outfit. A white angora beret was perched at a rakish angle atop her head.

Remer got out of the car to open the door for her, but tripped and fell right on the ground.

Emily laughed. "Oh, you're falling for me, are you?"

She was so good-natured that he forgot to be embarrassed. The two young people chatted easily during the afternoon ride and Mildred silently congratulated herself for being an excellent matchmaker. A few days later, Remer telephoned Emily.

"Would you like to go to the picture show Thursday night?"

She agreed, more out of politeness than real interest. But when Thursday night came, Remer Crum didn't show up. Emily was philosophical and not the least bit concerned. Bessie, however, didn't bother to hide her disapproval.

"Well, for goodness sake," she said, using her strongest language, and pursed her lips tight.

About a week later, Remer called again. "I'd like to take you to the picture show Saturday night. Can you go?"

"Well, what happened to you last Thursday?" she asked, barely concealing her amusement. "I thought we were going then."

There was a long silence. Then, in a sheepish voice, he said, "Oh, my gosh." He then explained that he'd been in the Finchers' living room when he'd called her and that the other boys, along with the Fincher girls, had come into the room as he hung up the telephone. "We got to talking and I . . . just forgot."

He sounded so sorry that Emily couldn't help but forgive him. She went to the movies with him that Saturday night and truly enjoyed the evening. They began seeing each other regularly. She found herself drawn to this young man with whom she could spend hours just talking.

Seven

A Trip to Mexico and a Wedding

In spite of her initial misgivings, Bessie Fisher quickly grew fond of Remer Crum. She thought he was charming and considerate and she was pleased that Emily was seeing him. Orr also took to the young man. Sometimes the two of them would sit and talk and Orr would pass on his philosophy of making a living. "You can buy stocks and bonds and all that sort of thing and they'll go up and they'll go down. But if you want to succeed, you buy some land and put your foot on it and hold it."

Fisher was a man who followed his own advice. He and Bessie still owned the property they had bought in Dekalb County. And they had recently purchased another farm on the outskirts of LaGrange.

Later that year, Remer left the Soil Conservation Department for work with the Georgia Highway Department. His new job was to survey and lay out new state highways. Emily continued to teach at Rosemont School and was pleased with the progress she'd made during her first year there. But a month before school was out, she was stricken with viral hepatitis. Weeks of bed rest were required for her recovery and Bessie stayed home with her every day to see that she got the care she needed. One afternoon there was a knock on the front door. Bessie opened it to find five of Emily's students on the doorstep.

"How is Mizz Fisher? Is she all right?"

They had walked all the way from Rosemont into town to check on their beloved teacher. Bessie sat them down and reassured them that Emily was going to be fine. Then she called Orr at work. He came right home and drove the children back to Rosemont.

$$\wp$$

Emily recovered completely and, when Bessie and Orr took a month-long motoring vacation to Mexico late in the summer, she and Remer and her girlfriend Elsie Kersey went along. They traveled across Texas and crossed into Mexico at San Antonio. Orr hired a guide to drive them around northern Mexico, but by the time they headed to Mexico City, he was driving them himself again. The days were long and hot and the travel over rough dirt tracks was difficult, but it was worth the discomfort for the opportunity to see places and people they'd only read about before. The three young people bounced along in the back seat, laughing and talking.

When the travelers reached Mexico City, they checked into a small hotel. After a few days of sightseeing, Remer announced he was going to Acapulco.

"I've heard about it. It's over on the coast and I've always wanted to see the Pacific Ocean."

The others were enjoying being off the road for a while and the relative comfort of their accommodations in the capital city. No one was interested in making the trip with him. So early one morning, Remer, by himself, caught a bus to Acapulco. The rickety little bus chugged along terrible roads, stopping every few minutes to pick up or deposit passengers. In no time it was crowded with people, pigs and chickens. It lurched around sharp curves on mountain roads where there weren't even flimsy guardrails between the bus and the sheer drops. Around him, people spoke a language he didn't understand and ate pungent food he'd never seen before. The smell of the exotic spices, combined with the odor of livestock and the pitching and lurching of the vehicle, made him queasy. It was with great relief that he finally left the bus at Acapulco just as darkness was falling.

Remer wasn't sure what he'd expected, but in 1938, Acapulco was not a particularly impressive place. The small community of houses and shops was clustered around a harbor, and steep mountains towered behind the town. Remer didn't see anything that looked like a hotel and he couldn't find a telephone with which to let Emily know he had made it safely to the coast. He was finally able to get something to eat in a small cantina. He spoke no Spanish, but with gestures and a lot of patience, he determined that there was no hotel available. There was, however, a local family who rented out rooms.

He found the house in question and, again through crude sign language, arranged for a room. It was a simple home, but they gave him a bed and a room to himself. For that, he was very grateful.

Remer had ripped his trousers on the bouncing bus ride and it was the only pair he'd brought with him. He asked, through gestures, if the woman of the house could mend them. She nodded that she could, so he went into his room, removed the trousers and, standing behind the door, handed them over to his hostess. In less than half an hour, she was back with the neatly mended pants.

Remer stayed several days in Acapulco. He and the son of the house in which he stayed were about the same age. Although they did not speak each other's language, they managed to communicate fairly well. The young man enjoyed showing Remer around his town. Remer finally got a close up view of the Pacific Ocean when the boy took him to La Quebrada. There every afternoon young men dove from the jagged, towering cliffs, timing their dives with the incoming waves to avoid landing in the potentially deadly shallows. It was the most impressive thing he'd ever seen anyone do.

Remer knew it was time to return to Mexico City, but he was determined to avoid a repeat of his earlier bus ride. At the Wells Fargo office he finally found a man who spoke a bit of English and learned that there was a mail plane that flew to Mexico City three times a week. It could accommodate three or four passengers. Remer bought a ticket then and there for the next day's flight.

The airstrip outside of town was little more than a dirt track. When the small plane took off the next morning, it rumbled down the strip, lifted off and headed straight for the mountains above Acapulco. At the last minute, or so it seemed to Remer, the plane gained just enough altitude to clear the highest peak. For the rest of the trip, the small airplane followed a bumpy route just above the mountaintops. When they landed in Mexico City two hours later, Remer had another experience to add to the list of things he wouldn't do again.

While Remer had been having a fine adventure, Emily and the others were growing more and more worried about him. They hadn't had so much as a phone call and were beginning to fear that something had happened to him. When the taxi dropped him off at the Mexico City hotel, he was greeted like a hero home from the wars.

After several weeks in a country where few people spoke their language, the travelers had grown accustomed to communicating with gestures and signs. So when Orr Fisher walked into the Mexico City post office, he didn't bother to ask if anyone there spoke English.

"Air mail stamp," he said very slowly in a loud voice. "Air mail stamp." He accompanied his words with the appropriate gestures. He spread his arms wide in an imitation of wings and zoomed around in a small circle.

The clerk observed all of this with a wooden expression. Then, in a dry voice, asked, "How many would you like, sir?"

The others teased Orr unmercifully about this episode. For many years to come, just mentioning the incident guaranteed laughter.

In LaGrange, anticipation was running high. It was well known that Remer had traveled to Mexico with Emily and her parents.

"They'll come back engaged or else!" Mildred Fincher declared.

But when Remer and Emily returned to LaGrange, there was no formal understanding and no ring on her finger. The Fincher girls were very disappointed. However, Remer knew he had found the woman with whom he wanted to spend the rest of his life. In November he bought a ring and summoned up the courage to propose. He was delighted when Emily accepted his offer of marriage. That delight was apparent when he wrote to his sister Florence:

> *LaGrange, Georgia*
> *December 28, 1938*
> *Dear Florence,*
> *Charles and Lily came up to spend Xmas with me. Charles stayed with me and Lily spent the weekend with Emily. Mr. & Mrs. Fisher were carried away with Lily's personality and manners.*
>
> *Florence, Emily and I are going to be married February 1st. I want you to get up the family history or whatever it is (the fact that is put in the paper when the announcement is made) and send it to me or Emily. I don't suppose it makes any difference. I know you know about these things. That is the date that we set for the marriage last night. I haven't talked to Mrs. Fisher about the details of the wedding. I will have Charles as my best man and three boys that work here in the wedding as groomsmen.*

The details do not make any difference other than the above two selections.

Emily is a fine girl and I love her as much as a man can love a woman. I know I am doing the right thing when I want to marry her.

She loves me the same way. I gave her a pretty little ring about a month ago. It is real pretty, too. It is a blue-white diamond and is .68 of a carat. The wedding band matches in material and design.

This is my first experience like this and I do not know what I am supposed to do. I will read Emily Post and find out however. I am more excited about everything than I have ever been.

I am getting along fine and send my love to Harry and the boys.

Lots of love,
Remer

The announcement is to be made Jan. 8ᵗʰ. Thanks for the Xmas gift. I like them very much.

§

Plans for the wedding progressed rapidly. Remer and Emily would marry on February 11ᵗʰ of the coming year. It was a very busy time for Emily. She was still teaching every day and much of the rest of her time was now taken up by the hundreds of details of the ceremony and reception.

Emily got a shock when she informed her employers of her upcoming marriage. She was told there was a rule that no teacher could be married. Her principal, a married *man*, gave her the news.

"Why don't you wait to get married until school's out?" he asked.

But Emily was not going to be persuaded to change her plans. On January 14, 1939, their engagement announcement appeared in the *LaGrange Daily News*. Emily was described as "possessing an appearance of unusual chic and a charming personality."

Being the groom, Remer had little to do with the event until the day of the wedding. He found other ways to occupy his time. One Saturday in late January, he and some friends went squirrel hunting. They loaded their shotguns and ammunition into Remer's green Studebaker and drove out in the country. They parked on the side of a dirt road and set off into the woods. Half an hour later, a barrage of gunshots erupted from the direction of the road. It sounded as if war had broken out. They ran the half-mile back and, as the car came into sight, they could see flames dancing in the back seat and smoke pouring from the windows. They weren't able to approach the car. Boxes of shotgun shells that had been left in the car kept exploding.

It wouldn't have mattered much if they'd gotten close to the vehicle since they had no means available to put out the fire. They could only stand and watch as the car was consumed. On the long walk back to town, they decided a careless cigarette ash must have started the fire, but the cause didn't seem very important at that point.

February 11th was Remer's birthday, and in 1939, it was also his and Emily's wedding day. It was a cold, clear Saturday and the marriage took place at noon in the First Baptist Church of LaGrange. The church was massed with floral arrangements, particularly Easter lilies whose fragrance filled the sanctuary. Although Remer's parents were sadly missing, all of his siblings attended the wedding. His brother Charles was his best man and his sister Lily was the bride's maid of honor. Emily, in a blush pink satin gown and tiered veil, was radiant. Remer, formal in striped trousers and a morning coat, was terrified. All he wanted was for the ceremony to be over and to be allowed to change into more comfortable clothes.

A formal luncheon for 65 guests at the nearby Colonial Hotel followed the ceremony. Afterwards, the couple, to Remer's great relief, changed from their formal clothes and left on their honeymoon. They drove to New Orleans in a car provided by Orr Fisher's auto agency. After a week at the Jung Hotel sampling the exotic sights and sounds of the Crescent City, it was time to return to LaGrange and the everyday world.

§ⱺ

The newlyweds set up housekeeping in the Daniel Apartments on Broad Street. There were four units in the building. Emily and Remer rented the one upstairs on the right. It had a bedroom, a kitchen, a living room and, their favorite feature, a small porch off the living room. They put a couple of chairs and a small table on the porch and could sit and watch the activity on Broad Street below. In the spring and summer they were sheltered from view by the leafy oak trees that lined the street. It was almost like living in a tree house.

Thanks to Bessie Fisher, Emily and Remer didn't have to buy furniture immediately or beg for bits and pieces from relatives. Bessie had become friendly with a young couple from Chicago who lived across the street from her for several years. Just before Emily and Remer's wedding, the young man was transferred back to Illinois.

The couple had recently purchased all new maple furniture for their bedroom, living room and dining room, but the shipping expense prevented their moving it to Chicago. When Bessie heard that, she asked them, "Why not let Emily and Remer take care of it for you? They'll take real good care of it. And when you get settled there and have enough money for shipping, they will send it to you."

The couple agreed and the newlyweds suddenly acquired an apartment full of almost-new furniture. They also assumed the payments on a stove and refrigerator that the other couple was buying on time. Emily and Remer were conscientious in their care of the furniture left with them. They treated it as if each piece was made of glass. Emily polished it weekly. Over the next year, they wrote to the couple several times to see if they were ready to have their furniture shipped to them. Each time the reply was "Not yet." Finally a letter came from Chicago, advising that they didn't think they were going to be able to have the furniture shipped to them after all. The expense was just too great. They asked that Emily and Remer sell their things and send the money to them. Rather than find other buyers, Emily and Remer purchased the furniture themselves.

Because of the unfortunate burning of the Studebaker, the Crums did not own a car when they were first married. The Department of Transportation provided Remer with a vehicle for his work, but for a short while the couple had to make do with a bicycle. It was a less than desirable form of transportation for two people. One evening they were invited to play bridge with Charlotte and Russell Redding. The Reddings' apartment was five or six blocks away. Remer pedaled and Emily sat on the narrow passenger seat in back. It was a rough and bumpy trip there and back. After that, Emily declared there would be no more bicycling for her. She would walk instead.

Emily had resigned from Rosemont School when she and Remer married, but she did not enjoy being idle. She decided to teach speech and drama to individual students in her home. However, she and Remer had been settled into their new home only a few weeks when her former principal called her. They had, he told her, made certain arrangements that would allow her to return to her teaching job. But Emily was not sure now that was what she wanted. She told him she planned to instruct individual children in her home. He countered with a suggestion that she work as a substitute teacher for the county school system and she agreed.

Emily had expected she would be called once or twice a week as a substitute. Instead, she found herself working every day, traveling all over the district. After two months, she decided it was too much work for the meager amount of money they were paying her and had her name removed from the substitute teacher list.

She returned to her original plan and began teaching speech and drama in her home. As word of her skill spread, Mr. Young at the Callaway Textile Mills contacted her. The county's largest employer, Callaway ran schools on the grounds for the children of the employees and Young recruited Emily to work for them, teaching speech and drama. She took the job and, within a few months, her students were performing all over town. The Rotary Club, the Lions Club and other civic organizations took advantage of this new resource and frequently presented programs featuring Emily's students.

In 1941, Emily and her friend Emelyn Goolsby discovered marionettes. The wooden puppets and the way the figures could be moved by manipulating the strings fascinated them. They grew so interested that they eventually constructed their own marionettes and wrote plays for them. They even enlisted some of Emily's students to provide voices for the puppets and do the stage-managing. When everything was ready, they scheduled their first public performance at the local Women's Club. It was to be held on a Saturday afternoon so that all the nannies could bring their young charges. Emelyn and Emily went around to the merchants in town and charmed them into putting posters in their windows to advertise the show.

When the big day arrived, the young women were ready. They'd constructed a stage for the marionettes and had arranged a few chairs at the back of the hall for the nannies. The children, they anticipated, would sit on the floor near the stage. Emily waited at the door to collect admission—25 cents for adults and 10 cents for children. Emelyn made a last minute check of the stage set up.

They were taken completely by surprise at the number of people who showed up for the performance. Child after child, accompanied by nanny or parent, streamed through the door. Emily could see they were in trouble. Leaving Emelyn to handle the door, she gathered up several of her students and hurried across the street to the First Baptist Church. There they fetched chairs from the classroom where Emily taught Sunday school and lugged them back to the Women's Club. Even with the additional chairs, some of the adults still had to stand.

The children were enthralled by the puppet show. Many of them had never seen anything like it before. Some of the younger ones even walked up to the stage and tried to talk to the marionettes. By any yardstick, their show was a roaring success. But their first production was to be their last. When the last child left the club, Emily and Emelyn collapsed into two of the chairs, completely exhausted. They decided, then and there, that there would be no more marionette shows. It was simply too much work.

Emily and Remer became good friends with another couple in their apartment building, Fritz and Myrtle Wagner. They were engaging people from interesting families. Fritz was the grandson of legendary Georgia writer Joel Chandler Harris. Myrtle's sister was a nurse who had married a Japanese doctor and lived in far away Hawaii.

It was Myrtle who first came to Emily's mind that Sunday afternoon in December 1941. She and Remer had purchased another car by then and were taking the usual after-church ride when news of the Pearl Harbor attack was announced on the radio. They rushed back to the apartment to be with their friends.

Fortunately, Myrtle's sister and her husband had not been hurt. But World War II had begun and life had changed forever. The focus of the nation had changed as well. Young, fit and childless, Remer knew he would serve. The only questions were where and how.

Eight

The War and Life Half a World Away

"I think I could be a navigator," Remer told Emily. "The Army Air Corps may be the place for me."

He wrote a letter to the Air Corps office in Atlanta, inquiring about joining up. However, the same day he received a response back from them setting up an interview, another letter arrived from the Department of the Navy. The Navy offered him a two-year contract as a civilian engineer rebuilding the portions of Pearl Harbor that had been destroyed in the December 7th attack.

Remer considered his options. While he was more than willing to do either job, he reasoned that he'd have to go through a certain amount of training to become a navigator. But he was already an engineer. That meant he could start doing the important work immediately. His decision was made.

In June of 1942, while the Battle of Midway was raging, he left for Hawaii. He boarded a Southern Pacific train in LaGrange and made the long trip across the southwest to Los Angeles. There he changed trains and continued up the coast to San Francisco. Three days later, he walked on board the U.S.S. America. Before the war, the liner had been the largest passenger ship afloat. Now that it had been taken over by the Navy, it had been transformed into a troop transport. Remer made the five-day trip to Hawaii with 25,000 other men.

He rented an apartment with two other men in Honolulu and spent his days overseeing the numerous repair and new construction projects for the Navy. Back in LaGrange, Emily continued her teaching at Callaway Mills. She gave up the apartment where she and Remer had spent three happy years and moved back into her parents' home. The maple furniture was stored in their basement. Being apart was hard, but they wrote regularly and knew the separation would not last forever.

In one late winter letter, Remer told Emily that the Navy was beginning a new program to bring civilian women workers to Hawaii. She could join him there if she were willing to work in the shipyard. Although she knew it would mean hard, physical labor and long hours, Emily didn't hesitate for a minute. Of course she would go! She didn't care what kind of work she'd have to do. A couple of weeks later, Remer sent her the Form 57, the official form she had to complete to apply to work in Hawaii. She began filling it out as soon as she received it.

Bessie and Orr Fisher did not want their only child to travel halfway around the world in wartime. They tried and tried to talk her out of what they considered to be a rash decision, but Emily would not be moved. They even recruited Dr. Willis Howard, minister of the First Baptist Church, to try and talk some sense into her. He met with Emily in his office.

"I don't believe you ought to go out there," he told her. "Neither do you parents. It could be very dangerous."

"Dr. Howard, you know I've been praying for a way to get to Remer since he left. And now it's come. Do you think I should not accept what the Lord has given me?"

He had little to say after that.

Emily sent in her Form 57 and, in a few months, she received her orders to go. In June of 1943, she arrived in Honolulu. It had been a year since she'd seen her husband and theirs was a joyful reunion.

Remer was still in the apartment he'd rented when he first came to Hawaii, but his two roommates had moved out when they learned that Emily was on her way. It was located only a block or so from Waikiki Beach and had begun life as a private home, but in recent years had been converted into three apartments. Theirs was the one at the back, consisting of one big room, a tiny kitchen and a bath. Emily thought it must have once been a sunroom because there were windows all the way around it. Now with the blackout in effect, heavy dark curtains lined all sides of the room. Remer warned her that, if even the tiniest chink of light were visible from their apartment, they'd receive a visit and a stern warning from a policeman.

On the first night in her new home, Emily settled down early to sleep, exhausted from the travel and the excitement of seeing her husband again. She was ripped from sleep by gunfire. It was so close and terrifying that she scrambled under the bed, sure that they were under attack. Remer calmed her and pulled her out. He explained that the Navy planes used Waikiki Beach to practice their strafing. It happened every night. Although she would not have believed it at the time, Emily eventually grew so accustomed to the nightly practice that she could sleep through it.

A few days later, Emily went to the naval base to learn what her new job would be. She was directed to a large room along with a hundred or so other women. They represented a wide cross section of Americans from all over the country. The one thing they had in common was that each had a husband who was a civilian employee of the Navy in Hawaii.

The women took their seats, exchanging nervous smiles. The first order of business was to determine who was best suited for the available jobs. A young man stood before them and asked questions to find out which of the women had experience in welding, electrical work or carpentry. Emily knew she had nothing to contribute in these areas. She'd hardly ever touched a tool her whole life. She shifted uncomfortably in her seat as he took the names of the experienced women and sent them off to their new jobs. But her luck changed when the questions turned to education.

"Has anyone here ever gone to college?"

Emily was the only one who raised her hand. When the young man learned she not only attended college, but also graduated, he sent her to the Personnel Department.

"Ask for Mrs. Page."

Mrs. Page was a pleasant, middle-aged woman, who was slightly flustered when Emily found her.

"We've just started this female recruitment program," she told the younger woman. "That's what you'll be working on. But right now—oh, I haven't got things fixed up the way I want yet." She looked around the cluttered area. "Just sit in my office and do what you want for now. Read a book or something."

Emily was not a young woman who enjoyed doing nothing. "What I'd really like to do is write a little book of instructions so the ladies would know what to expect when they start out."

Mrs. Page gave her a big smile. "That's a great idea! Go down to the Art Department and get one of the boys there to work with you."

In a couple of weeks, Emily and the Art Department had produced a booklet that would be sent to thousands of young women over the next three years.[*]

The Crums both worked long days. Most of the civilian employees at Pearl Harbor worked six days a week. Often by the time they got home in the evenings, the store shelves would be nearly bare, but they made do with what they had. When they weren't working, they could usually be found outside enjoying the

---

[*] A few pages of that booklet are reproduced in the back of the book as an appendix.

warm weather. They loved going to beach. After a while, they became so tanned that they could pass as native Hawaiians.

Their apartment became a gathering place for Georgia servicemen whose ships docked there at the primary Pacific port. Friends from home would call when they arrived and were always welcome at Emily and Remer's place. When they left Hawaii, these friends often passed on the Crums' telephone number to their friends. Soon complete strangers were showing up at the Crums' apartment. Emily became accustomed to stretching meals for two to feed three or four. They never turned anyone away and Emily received more letters than she could count from mothers thanking her for her kindness to their sons.

One such visitor was Billy Eiland. He and his family had lived for years down the street from Emily's family in LaGrange. When his ship docked at Pearl, the first thing he did was call Emily. She was thrilled to hear from him, but sorry she hadn't had a bit more notice.

"I want you to come to dinner, but all I can make is scrambled eggs, bacon and grits."

He wasn't discouraged. "That sounds wonderful!"

A short time later he was at the Crums' apartment. It was a warm, wonderful night. They ate food that reminded them of kitchens back home and talked of family and mutual friends in soft, familiar Georgia accents. It was the last meal Billy Eiland would have with people he knew from before the war. He shipped out the next day and was killed soon after at Iwo Jima.

When news reached the islands about the battle, including the names of the ships involved, Emily was very concerned about Billy. She kept seeing him as the child he'd been, not the sailor he'd become. Finally she sent word to the Naval Hospital and asked that they post a note requesting that anyone who had information about Billy Eiland get in touch with her. A few days later she returned from work to find a solemn-faced young sailor sitting on her back porch. She knew the news was not going to be good. Over coffee, he told her that Billy had been killed at Iwo Jima. He even knew where her friend was buried and gave her directions to the grave.

Conrad Snell was another serviceman from Georgia. He had also recently become related to Emily. Just before shipping out to Hawaii, he had married her cousin Helen Pittman. Once he arrived at Pearl Harbor, he became a frequent visitor in the Crums' home, stopping by at least once a week. Conrad was more than a sailor; he was an accomplished artist. When Emily learned that he would be going to Iwo Jima for the clean up, she gave him the directions she'd received from the young sailor and asked that he paint a picture of Billy Eiland's grave. Weeks later, Emily received the canvas from him. It was a beautiful painting of the graveyard and Eiland's grave. She sent it on to Billy's family in LaGrange.

Emily and Remer were people who believed there was nothing they couldn't do if they set their minds to it. So when they decided to make some extra money by selling island art, they never hesitated. Emily carved designs in wooden blocks and Remer stamped pieces of cloth with brightly colored paint. They even got their friends involved and set up an assembly line in their living room, making and hanging the prints up to dry. They sold their creations to the service personnel who found them more attractive than the items they saw in the local souvenir shops. They were so successful with the prints that they decided to branch out. Bessie Fisher was an accomplished seamstress and Emily wrote and asked her to make a dozen plain white aprons. Bessie was happy to do so. When the aprons arrived in Hawaii, Remer and Emily adorned each one with a small stamped tropical design and sold them for $10 a piece.

The couple who rented the front apartment in their building, John Holliman and his wife, Ellen Wing Hong Holliman, became their good friends. The Crums and the Hollimans were famous for the parties they threw. The luaus were always held outdoors and everyone—friends, acquaintances, passersby—was welcome. The food was whatever they had available and a Victrola provided the music. Sometimes the entertainment was remarkable. Ellen Holliman was a professional dancer and had been giving Emily lessons. One afternoon, as the luau was in full swing, *Hula Hands* issued forth from the Victrola. Emily and Ellen climbed on a table and performed. Three young servicemen who had been walking down the street stopped to watch the grass-skirted dancers.

"Come join the party," a guest called out to them.

"We don't have time," one of the men answered. He lifted a home movie camera. "But could we take their picture?"

"Sure."

The serviceman filmed the two dancers for several minutes. When the music ended, another party guest asked him where he was from.

"Atlanta, Georgia."

"Georgia? You're not going to believe this! Emily's from Georgia."

She called Emily over, but rather than being pleased at meeting a fellow Georgian, the young man was disappointed. He had believed they were watching native Hawaiians dance.

"Oh, man, I just wasted 40 feet of film on a hula dancer from Georgia!"

When the holidays arrived, the young couple from LaGrange was especially conscious of just how far they were from home. They had an "Old Fashioned New England Thanksgiving Dinner" in a thatched-roof restaurant with no walls, sitting within sound of the surf. It wasn't like any Thanksgiving they'd ever known. And when the Christmas season arrived, they longed for cold weather and the comfort of home. But greetings and gifts from friends and family helped a lot. One of the most special came from Remer's sister Lily. She made them a fruitcake. A teacher in Cordele, she baked the seasonal treat in a metal chalk box she'd brought home from school and sanitized. When it was done, she poured Welch's grape juice over it to keep it moist. Then she put on the lid and sent it to Hawaii. The chalk box made a perfect mailing container, but it took a couple of weeks to reach its destination. In thanking her, Remer declared it was the best fruitcake he'd ever had. Lily always wondered if that might have been because the grape juice fermented on the long trip to Hawaii.

Emily enjoyed her job. With her outgoing personality and her love of people, she was perfectly suited for the position. Civilian workers who wanted their wives or fiancées to join them came to Emily for help. She walked them through the process, making sure they met all the requirements. She also was responsible for meeting the women when they arrived.

There was never any advance notice of the ships' arrivals. When they docked, Emily would be called and would go and meet the new female workers as they left the ships. She would then take them to their husbands, a task that was sometimes easier said than done. Since no one ever told the men when to expect their wives, they weren't always available when the women arrived. It wasn't unusual for Emily and her driver to be out in the blackout after midnight, with one or two wives in tow, searching for their husbands. But it was all worth the effort when she brought a couple together again.

§⌐

When the war ended, Emily and Remer returned to Georgia for a visit. They visited Remer's family in Cordele and stayed for a week with Bessie and Orr in LaGrange. The Fishers had moved from the house on North Greenwood to the farm they'd purchased outside of town. It was a happy interlude for Emily and Remer, a time of renewing friendships and enjoying all the things they'd missed while they were away.

One of the things they'd hoped to accomplish while they were home was purchasing a car to take back to Hawaii. But in 1946, this was nearly impossible. The demand was so high that auto manufacturers couldn't keep pace with it. But Orr Fisher was not going to be defeated. He managed to get them a car—and not just any car. Orr found them a shiny, brand new 1946 Dodge.

They left LaGrange and drove their new car to Atlanta where they stayed a few more days. Whether it was Orr's example or just something he'd wanted to do, Remer looked into the real estate market there, and he and Emily purchased their first piece of property. It was located on Northside Drive in north Atlanta. When they came back to Georgia for another visit in 1948, they purchased a second piece of property on Hoke Street, close to the first.

The Crums lived in Hawaii for four more years. They moved from the one-room apartment to a duplex on the naval base, very close to Hickam Field. This time, there was no strafing practice, but planes did take off about every fifteen minutes—right over their house. At night, the lights illuminated their bedroom like the morning sun. If they'd been foolish enough to stand on their roof, they'd have risked being struck by a wing.

Emily tried to get used to this new distraction. A neighbor told her not to worry.

"Why those power lines in front of your house would stop a plane before it hit the house."

Emily glanced at the few wires strung between the power poles and found no comfort in her friend's reassurances.

The Crums might have stayed in Hawaii—it was a lovely place to live—but they missed their families 4,500 miles away. In 1950, they decided to return to Georgia.

NINE

THE MAKING OF A HOME AND THE BEGINNING OF A DREAM

Back home, Remer took a job as a project engineer with Robert and Company, an Atlanta architectural and engineering firm. His first project with the company took him and Emily to Rossville, Georgia, a small town just over the state line from Chattanooga, Tennessee. Once again, they set out to meet their neighbors and find ways to become part of their new community. Remer planned and oversaw the building of an addition to the Peerless Woolen Mills.

After a year, the project was complete. The folks at Robert and Company were pleased with his work and ready to send him on to another job in another place. And, after that, there would be another and another. But Emily was not willing to go on. She longed to find one place, put down roots and stay there. Remer agreed. He resigned from Robert and Company and they returned to Atlanta.

Emily and Remer weren't sure where they wanted to live permanently. There was an old house on the Hoke Street property they'd bought five years before and they moved in there temporarily. It was not a large place, but they didn't need much room. Remer decided to try his hand in real estate development. He built a service station on the Northside Drive property and leased it to the Texaco Oil Company. This would be the first of many such ventures.

Orr and Bessie Fisher were ready to slow down a bit. With their only daughter back in the United States, they wanted to spend as much time with her and her husband as possible. In late 1950, Orr sold the automobile dealership in LaGrange, and he and Bessie moved to Atlanta. They decided to rent a house until they found one they wanted to buy. They drove around the city and followed up on ads in the newspaper. One of these ads was for a house in Ansley Park. The Fishers liked the place as soon as they saw it. And they liked the owners when they met them. The Callahans were leaving the country for a year and wanted to rent their house while they were gone. As the two couples wandered through the big, comfortable rooms, conversation turned to relatives, friends and acquaintances, as it so often does in the south. It was with a mixture of surprise and delight that they discovered the Callahans had once lived only a few doors down from some of Bessie's relatives in Birmingham. That knowledge provided the couples with an almost instant kinship and sealed the deal.

Bessie and Orr returned the favor by showing exceptional kindness to the Callahans' son. The young man was in college and remained in the United States while his parents were out of the country, so the Fishers opened their home to him. Nearly every weekend during the school year, he came "home" and stayed in the room that had been his for so many years. The Fishers treated him like family.

When the year's lease was up, the Callahans began planning their return home and Bessie and Orr moved temporarily into the house on Hoke Street with Emily and Remer. Even though they were able to divide it into two apartments, the house was small and conditions were cramped. They were all relieved when, a few months later, the Fishers bought a house up on a hill on The Byway in the Ansley Park section of town.

℘

Emily and Remer continued to acquire property over the next few years. In addition to developing and managing his own properties, Remer took occasional jobs overseeing other construction projects. For a while, he even worked for the Corps of Engineers, building facilities at Fort Benning and Fort Gordon. But by 1954, he abandoned working for other people and concentrated on building up his own real estate and development company.

The Crums joined St. Mark United Methodist Church and quickly became active in the life there. They bought a lot on Paces Ferry Road, just inside the village of Vinings, north of Atlanta. In 1956, Remer drew up plans for a house and hired contractors to build it. Their friends couldn't believe that they were serious about moving so far out of town. In fact, the word "boondocks" came up more than once. But the Crums loved the location and were excited about owning their own home.

Emily oversaw every phase of the construction, sitting in the back yard in a lawn chair and watching as the work was done, every day, all day long. One of the special features Remer had designed was a huge fieldstone fireplace in the family room. When the day came for the stone to be laid, a truck full of workmen arrived at the house. They worked on other projects all morning. Then it was time to begin laying the fieldstone. Only one old man came in the house to work. His three young companions stayed in the truck, drinking beer. Emily watched uneasily as the frail old fellow began placing the flat stones atop each other. Instead of the usual straight lines, the stones he set in place dipped and waved across the expanse of the big hearth. Finally she could stand it no longer. She went to the truck and rapped on the window until one of the men opened the door.

"The man inside is laying all the stones crooked. You better get in there and fix it."

Her voice was stern—she'd used the same tone when teaching school and the workmen sensed the steel behind her words. They piled out of the truck and went inside the half-built house where they began disassembling the crooked fireplace. By the time they left at the end of the day, the hearth and chimney had been rebuilt, the lines straight and true.

It was around this time that Emily discovered embroidery and needlework. From the moment she threaded her first needle and stretched her first fabric in a hoop, she was hooked. She loved the precision demanded of her and the delicate beauty she could produce. She joined the Dogwood Chapter of the Embroiderers Guild and became very active in the group. From that day forth, Emily was rarely seen without a needle in her hand or very nearby.

The Crums loved to entertain. They often hosted dinners for friends from their church. And their hospitality was not limited to adults. Nieces and nephews were always welcome in their home. One of the visitors they most enjoyed was Suzanne Crum. The daughter of Remer's younger brother Charles, Suzanne began spending a week or two each summer with them when she was only eight years old. Her first summer visit was in 1957. She never missed a year after that until she was grown and married. Her aunt and uncle became almost second parents to her.

One year when she was very young, Emily and Remer took her to an outdoor theater production of *Babes in Toyland*. Remer always did his best to see that Suzanne had exactly what she wanted, so when she asked for cotton candy from the refreshment stand, he was determined to get it for her. He took his place at the end of the long line. Emily and Suzanne stood to one side as he inched forward toward the counter. They could hear music and laughter and knew the show had started, but the line moved very slowly. Nearly an hour passed before Remer reached the counter and made his purchase. They missed the first half of the show, but Suzanne had her cotton candy.

Emily always had activities planned for her niece and tried to include other children her age. She never had any trouble entertaining them. Sometimes she would pull out the grass skirts and leis from her years in Hawaii and give the little girls hula lessons. Perhaps Suzanne's favorite activity was shopping with her aunt. They would go to Rich's department store and spend hours there. Suzanne always brought $10 with her from home and she managed to buy gifts to take back to every member of her family from that amount. Emily always had to make sure the little girl got something for herself as well.

In 1963, the Crums purchased some property off Five Forks-Trickum Road in Gwinnett County, northeast of Atlanta. They built a lake and a little rustic cabin and cleared some land where Remer was determined to have an apple orchard. In March, he took some time away from his office and, with some hired help, planted 700 apple trees on the Gwinnett property. It was backbreaking work, made more difficult by the knowledge that the trees would not produce an acceptable crop for five or six years. When they'd finally finished, he was exhausted and glad to return to the relative ease of his office.

A couple of days later, Emily called him at work.

"A truck just delivered a hundred more apple trees."

"What?" Remer did not sound pleased. "I didn't order any more trees!"

"Well, they're here. The nursery said these were a bonus because you had bought so many from them."

Remer's voice rose. "That's ridiculous! I don't want any more trees. I can't even think about planting any more trees. You call that nursery and tell them to come back and pick up—"

"April Fool!" Emily said sweetly.

Remer had such a headache after that phone call that he had to send someone out to buy aspirin.

℘

In the fall of that year, Emily and Remer had exciting plans to make. November 26th would be her parents' 50th wedding anniversary and Emily was determined to make it a very special celebration. The Crums planned an afternoon reception at their Paces Ferry home. On the special day, the house shone with candlelight and crystal. Golden roses and snapdragons graced the tables. In the guestroom, Emily had laid her mother's bridal outfit on the bed for all to see. Between 3:00 and 6:00 that afternoon, over a hundred people came by to share the happy occasion. Cards and letters and telephone calls flooded the house. Fred and Irene Main, friends of the Crums from their days in Honolulu, even had two fresh orchid leis flown in from Hawaii. Bessie wore one and Emily the other. It wasn't until some weeks later, after Emily had sent the Mains photos from the party that she discovered the second lei had been intended for her father to wear.

Emily loved to make things and could be quite inventive in her choice of gifts. Friends and relatives had learned to happily anticipate receiving one of her special creations when birthdays or holidays approached. In 1965, Suzanne Crum turned sixteen. A large package was delivered to her home in Cordele. She opened it with excitement, then just stared for a moment at the contents. Nestled in the box was a very large, bright red Styrofoam watermelon slice. Suzanne was puzzled. Why would Aunt Emily and Uncle Remer send her such a gift? True, her hometown of Cordele was the Watermelon Capital of the World and she had recently taken part in the Watermelon Queen pageant, but she still couldn't imagine what they thought she would do with a two-foot long Styrofoam watermelon slice. She bent forward to examine it more closely. That's when she noticed the seeds were not painted on. Each one was a dollar bill, painstakingly folded to the size of a watermelon seed and imbedded in the foam.

Although he was officially retired, Orr Fisher still managed the property he and Bessie owned in several states and kept up with the real estate business. He was very much aware of how the face of Atlanta was changing. When Interstate 85 was constructed northeast of the city in the early sixties, it cut right through the Fisher farm on Clairmont Road. Divided by a major highway, the property was no longer viable for farming. Orr sold the acreage east of the ex-pressway to a developer, who turned it into a residential sub-division, but he held on to the property on the west side of the highway.

Over the next few years, he was approached numerous times about selling the farm, but he refused the offers that came his way. He felt very strongly that he should hold on to the land he and Bessie had bought just after coming to Atlanta so many years before. He couldn't, however, ignore the growth of the region or the importance of the land's location. He began thinking that he might be able to earn some money from the property and still keep it in the family. He wouldn't relinquish ownership, but he was willing to consider leasing the land for development.

Jon R. Gray, known as Dick, was one of the bright young Atlantans emerging in the sixties, poised to make his mark and change the city. In 1961, he'd begun his own mechanical engineering firm, but he wanted more than that. After marrying Martha Kemp in 1963, he entered law school at Emory University, while remaining at the helm of his company. It was more than a full time job. His firm now had 100 employees and 40 trucks. Gray attended classes whenever he could schedule them, some during the day, some in the evenings. He studied every chance he got, plucking the odd fifteen minutes here, half an hour there, from his busy day. During those years he rarely slept more than three hours a night.

He received his law degree and passed the bar in 1965. He and Martha bought a rambling house on Riverside Drive and he opened his own law practice where he specialized in corporate and real estate law.

One morning Gray left his Sandy Springs home for Atlanta where he would meet with some clients about a real estate deal. He circled the northern edge of the city, then turned south on Interstate 85, heading for downtown. Traffic moved sluggishly and, during his ride, he passed the Clairmont Road exit and reflected that the property on the northwest side of the expressway was conspicuously underdeveloped. In fact, the rolling wooded land looked out of place amid the blooming subdivisions and small office parks. The sight of so much unused land set him to thinking. In fact, he continued to ponder the situation and mentioned it during his morning meeting.

"Yeah, I know just where you mean," said Bill Woodward, a local real estate broker. "Guy named T. Orr Fisher owns that land. But he won't sell. He'll talk to you about it all you want, but that's all. You might as well forget it."

But Gray didn't forget it. The land was, he had decided, the ideal location for a multi-use office park. He himself lived north of Atlanta and spent 45 minutes every morning and 45 minutes every afternoon commuting to and from the city. And that was on good days when there were no accidents to tie traffic up even more. He calculated he spent 7 hours a week commuting. Over the next 25 years, he would waste 4 years sitting in traffic. He hated the idea and was willing to bet there were a lot more people who felt the same way. It was time to offer commuters an alternative.

A few days later, he asked Woodward to introduce him to Fisher. The two men met in Hardy Kilgore's office at General Apartments, Inc. Woodward had been right. Fisher was not interested in an outright sale of his property. He would, however, consider a ground lease. That was all Gray needed to hear. He started right then to construct a plan. Hardy Kilgore and Marvin Ingram joined him in developing the plan for the office park which would be called Century Center.

The first order of business was determining the property's worth. It consisted of 100 acres, Fisher had declared, and was worth three million dollars. Gray arranged for the land to be surveyed and the result surprised them a bit. It was 88 acres, not 100. They took this information back to Mr. Fisher and suggested he change the value he'd set on the land, but he would not budge. He'd said the property was worth three million dollars and he still believed that. They could proceed on that basis or not. Gray and the others decided to move forward.

Closing the deal took quite a while. It was a very complicated situation and each side was being extremely careful. Mr. Fisher wasn't especially fond of attorneys. In fact, he wanted to go ahead without one, but Dick Gray felt that was unwise. He kept after the older man and finally got Fisher to hire his own attorney. Then began the weary business of proposals and counter proposals. One side would send a proposed agreement to the other. Then the receiving side would make changes and send it back for consideration. Tedious though it was, they were gradually narrowing their differences. By the fall of 1968, they were close enough to an agreement that Gray felt he could leave the city for a short time. He flew to Las Vegas to attend a Home Builders Association convention. He'd been in the desert only a day when he got a call from his office. Mr. Fisher's attorney, after reviewing the latest draft of the proposed agreement, wanted to completely change the initial agreement or he would pull his client out of the deal. Gray flew home on the first available flight. The next morning he met with Orr Fisher himself. Gray was tired and frustrated.

"Your lawyer wants to change the deal. I'll tell you truth, we're ready to just walk away from this."

Orr Fisher had always been a man of his word and he wasn't about to change at this point in his life. He had not known of his lawyer's communication with Gray and didn't agree with it. He had made a deal and he would stand by it.

On November 6, 1968, Orr and Bessie signed the 90-year lease agreement with Gray, Ingram and Kilgore. In the simplest terms, the developers agreed to lease the land from the Fishers. The land was valued at 3 million dollars and the lessees agreed to pay 6% of that amount annually for the first ten years, 7% for the second ten years, 8% for the next, 9% for the next and 10% for the remaining years. Now it was up to Dick Gray and his partners to put the project together.

TEN

A GREAT LOSS

As soon as the lease agreement was signed, Dick Gray began working to have the property rezoned from rural to light commercial. There were objections, of course, from residents opposed to any kind of commercial encroachment, but things seemed to be going smoothly enough. In the summer of 1969, he took a short vacation in the Florida Keys. One morning as he walked through the streets of Marathon, his eye was caught by a headline showing through the window of a newspaper box. There had been serious flooding in Dekalb County, Georgia. There was a picture of a house with water up to the roof and, when he got close enough to read the caption, he learned that the house was located on Clairmont Way. Gray's heart sank. Clairmont Way was a residential street just across Clairmont Road from the proposed site of Century Center. He knew without question that his zoning request had just died.

Back in Atlanta, Gray pulled the rezoning request off the County Commission agenda and hired a local firm to conduct a hydrological study of the property. He learned the primary reason Peachtree Creek flooded so often in that area after heavy rains was that the waterway was filled with debris and beaver dams. The company had the obstructions removed and widened the banks, then refiled and got the zoning changes they needed.

Two months later, ground was broken for the Century Center Office Park. The event was celebrated with a lavish party at the Commerce Club on July 22nd. Construction was expected to take seven years and would combine high rise and single story buildings. Many of the natural features of the land would be left untouched. Gray and his partners wanted this development to be as much like a park as possible—a quiet, calm place where people could work in peace and drive home a short distance for lunch. Bessie and Orr were pleased with the developers' vision for their land and were looking forward to seeing the first building go up.

℘

In April of 1969, the Fishers had sold their house on The Byway and moved into the luxury Buckhead high-rise apartment building, the Georgian Manor. It was a fine place to live, convenient to everything, including their daughter's home, with the bonus of a pool and clubhouse on the ground floor.

The building was a very popular place for parties and other gatherings. The Fishers' friends often asked them to arrange for the use of the building's amenities for special functions and Bessie and Orr were happy to help. That was the case on a hot day in the last week of August of 1969. The daughter of one of Emily and Remer's friends was getting married and the reception was to be held in the Georgian Manor clubhouse that evening. Remer and Emily were helping to get the room ready and Orr had come downstairs to watch them set up and decorate the tables.

When Emily took a break, she noticed her father was not looking well.

"I don't feel good," he said in answer to her question. "I'm going back upstairs."

A few minutes later, a friend came running into the clubhouse.

"Your mother wants you upstairs right now! Your father's sick!"

They hurried up to the apartment where Orr Fisher was half-sitting, half-lying on the living room sofa. The color had drained from his face and Bessie told them he was horribly nauseated.

"We have to get him to the hospital," she said.

They managed to get him downstairs and into the car and Remer drove them the short distance to the Piedmont Hospital emergency room. Orr was immediately admitted and whisked off into the treatment area, leaving Bessie, Emily and Remer in the waiting room. After what seemed like hours, word finally came that he had suffered a heart attack and had been placed in the hospital's intensive care unit.

That day began the longest week any of them ever knew. Every morning, Emily and Remer drove Bessie to the hospital where they all spent the day in the waiting room. Every two hours, either Bessie or Emily was allowed to sit with Orr for fifteen minutes. He could have only one visitor at a time. The rest of the time, they waited, trying to keep each other's spirits up and praying for good news.

By the end of a week, it seemed to the family that Orr's condition was slightly improved. Remer was encouraged enough to have his wife and mother-in-law go to the hospital alone while he drove the thirty miles to Gwinnett County to check on the apple orchard. Two hours passed, then Bessie and Emily heard the alarm bell and the Code Blue announcement that they'd learned meant an emergency in the intensive care unit. Emily was suddenly sure that her father was that emergency. When, a few minutes later, the doctor brought them the news that Orr had died, she accepted it as something she already knew.

Emily called the Gwinnett County Police and asked them to send an officer to Five Forks Road to let Remer know about her father's death. Remer had been cleaning up around the lake house when a police car came into view. The moment he saw it, he knew that they must be bringing bad news. When they told him that Orr Fisher was dead, his only thought was to get back to town to help his wife and Bessie. He drove so fast that he arrived before the two women left the hospital.

The next few days were a blur of grief and arrangements. Orr Fisher was a much-loved man. When he died at age 83, the family received calls and condolences from hundreds of people. He was buried at Westview Abbey in Atlanta.

℘

Not only was Orr's death a terrible emotional shock to his family, it nearly spelled their financial ruin. True to his philosophy, Orr Fisher had continued to buy property. On paper, he was a very wealthy man. But that was on paper. Land is not necessarily a liquid asset. At his death, the family faced a $187,000 estate tax liability for federal, Georgia and South Carolina taxes. They did not have enough cash to cover these debts and Bessie, Emily and Remer had some hard decisions to make.

They all felt it was important to keep as much of the property intact as they possibly could, but drastic measures were called for. Finally they decided to sell off a few acres of land. Then Emily and Remer put their own savings and holdings into the pot with the capital Bessie had. Still they didn't have enough cash. They financed the rest and paid it off over the next ten years. But they felt they were successful. The Clairmont Road property remained intact.

℘

1970 was a difficult economic time. The boom of the sixties appeared to be over. Hardy Kilgore had already dropped out of the

Century Center deal when Marvin Ingram and Dick Gray formed the Commercial and Industrial Property Company and set out to find financing for their project. Not only did they have to locate financing, they had to find a good deal. They knew what they did at this point would have long-ranging implications. It would affect the rent structure of the future office buildings for years to come. It was imperative that they keep their obligations relatively low in order to keep the rental rates competitive.

Gray set out to find backers. He had, by now, left his law practice and was devoting all his time to the Century Center project. He had a list of 58 different financial institutions throughout the country and was ready to visit each one personally, if that was what it took. The project itself was complicated since Ingram and Gray only had the rights to the use of the land. That meant that, if anything happened to the project, the landowners would have first claim. Mortgage holders and contractors would come second.

Another stumbling block was Dick Gray's track record—or lack of it. At 29 years old, with no experience putting together a project of this size, Gray could hardly expect to inspire confidence on the part of the real estate mortgage people that he approached.

"You'll never be able to do this," he was told by more than one potential investor.

That was challenge enough for Gray. He would not be told he couldn't do something. He finally found the financing he sought at Continental Mortgage Investors in Coral Gables, Florida. A man there named Ron Holiday decided to take a chance on the young developer.

"You know," he said, "I believe you can do it."

Dick Gray believed it, too.

Ingram and Gray contracted with Newhaus and Taylor, a firm of Texas architects, to design the first structure in Century Center—an eleven-story office building of white pre-cast concrete and chrome reflective glass. Next they began the tedious work of grading the property. They moved over two and a half million yards of dirt in the course of several months.

In the first week of July, 1970, their grading contractor unexpectedly filed for bankruptcy. When the news reached Gray, he knew his project was in danger of being thrown seriously off schedule. The only solution he could find was a radical one. He bought the grading company himself—not an easy task over a long July 4th weekend, but he managed to do it. They didn't lose a single day's work.

Construction on the first building began in the summer of 1970. It would tower over the Interstate and be known as the 2200 Building. Its stark white color became the theme of the project and would eventually be echoed throughout the rest of the park. Several of the single story buildings were built soon after that. The developers tried to leave standing as many of the old trees as possible and supplemented the older plantings with new ones. Willows, silver maples and magnolias lined the roads and parking lots. In addition to Peachtree Creek, which meandered through the development, a two-acre lake was added to the property to intensify the feeling of working close to nature.

Marvin Ingram dropped out of the project in late 1970. Dick Gray reinvented the company as Gray Properties, Inc., and moved forward.

Century Center was vigorously marketed. The public relations firm that was hired touted both the amenities that were already in place and those that would come. The park would provide secretarial services, banking, a postal substation, and pick up and delivery for dry-cleaning. There would be restaurants, a ticket and travel agency, office supply facilities, private helicopter and limousine services, and even a decorating service for individual design of executive offices. Eventually a high rise hotel would be erected there as well. Their custom brochure, hardbound and letter-sized, looked more like a book than a marketing pamphlet. It emphasized the property's history and the company's dedication to keeping in touch with the land.

"From the very outset," it read, "we worked from a careful master plan designed to ensure that this magnificent site would stay much the same as it was when Mr. T. Orr Fisher farmed it. We've spared every fine old tree we possible could and replanted where we had to. We've added a two-acre, landscaped lake, which will be home for some of the happiest ducks in Atlanta. We've widened and landscaped Peachtree Creek so it will stay clean, clear and deep. We've even made a park along its banks. This is a total special green world apart from the tangle of noise and neon that surrounds most office parks."

Their philosophy was further reflected in the letter they sent to interested tenants:

Dear Prospective Tenant:

At Century Center, we are in the "people business"—not of just providing office space of concrete and steel, but in the business of creating and maintaining an environment.

We offer a refreshingly new concept—one that places high priority on the employee's contentment and attitude. When you move to Century Center, you will discover your employee morale and productivity will be increased, and you will have less employee turnover.

The architecture and landscaping are solid evidences of the ingenuity of this new environment. The ownership, management, security forces, grounds and engineering staffs are located at the Center to ensure continued maintenance. Just pick up the phone, and we are at your service.

Move to Century Center where we have built as you would for yourself. We pledge our unconditional guarantee to render every service required by you as our tenant in an efficient and professional manner.
Sincerely,
Jon Richard Gray, Owner

By the end of the next year, the 2200 Building was completed and beginning to fill. The first major tenant was the Bank Building Corporation of St. Louis, Missouri. Others followed, but the poor economic times couldn't be ignored and the rate of rental was nowhere as brisk as Gray had hoped.

The country was now in an acknowledged recession and the depressed economy did not encourage expansion. Dick Gray was able to hold on, but his financial backer, Continental Mortgage, hit hard times and wanted out. It took some scrambling, but after a while Gray managed to find alternative financing that would enable him to buy out Continental. He was feeling fairly accomplished at pulling it off when the deal hit a snag. The economy had been slowly improving and Continental Mortgage no longer wanted out of the Century Center project. In fact, they refused to go through with the buyout.

Gray was faced with a dilemma. He couldn't back out of the agreement with his new lenders and Continental was refusing to close on the sale. Finally Gray Properties filed an injunction against Continental Mortgage in Federal court where Judge Sidney Smith came down on the side of Gray Properties. It was, Smith declared, the first time he remembered someone had to be sued into taking their own money.

The legal detour brought on a time crunch. Gray had to close with his new lender before completing the buyout. Otherwise he would not have the money in hand to pay Continental. But he'd already been scheduled for minor surgery and didn't want to postpone it. On the day of the first closing, Dick Gray was still recuperating. The lawyers and secretaries came to his Riverside Drive home where, dressed in a bathrobe, he met with them and the closing was accomplished. The next day he paid Continental Mortgage their money and the buyout was complete.

ELEVEN

THE COMING OF AN ANGEL

Orr Fisher had been a remarkable, vibrant man and his absence left a huge void in the lives of his wife and daughter. They visited his grave at the Westview Abbey often and found that talking about him and sharing memories of the man helped with their grief. Remer felt the loss as well, but he was also busier than he'd ever been, trying to look after the Fishers' property while keeping up with his own business.

A few years after Orr's death, Bessie, Remer and Emily became aware of a problem that could threaten the Century Center development. In his will, Orr had established the Fisher Family Trust, the assets of which consisted of 15% of the undivided interest in the Clairmont Road land. The trust had 17 beneficiaries, all of whom were Fisher relatives. The Trust Company of Georgia Bank was named the corporate trustee and Emily and one of her cousins were appointed trustees. As the Century Center project began to grow, Bessie, Remer and Emily realized just how difficult it was going to be to have so many different owners of one piece of property. Every time a decision about the land and leases was made, all of them would have to be consulted. They debated it for weeks until they came to an inescapable conclusion. Something had to be done to change the arrangement.

Their first step was to have the property assessed. Once they had a definite value, they then determined what 15% of that figure was and set out to buy out the interest of the other beneficiaries. The three of them went to every single beneficiary of the trust and persuaded each one to agree to the buyout. The process took weeks and they logged hundreds of miles in their car, but they finally accomplished their goal and every one of the beneficiaries signed the agreement. The Fisher Family Trust continued, and does to this day, but its assets are in cash and investments rather than in land.

§

Building continued at Century Center and managing the complex was becoming a huge task. Gray Properties had their own janitorial and security staff. They also employed leasing people, designers and accountants.

In 1974, work began on the 17-story triangular building that would become the landmark structure of the park. On June 5th, 500 people, including Bessie Fisher and the Crums, attended the Topping Out Ceremony at Century Center. The bare bones of the structure were complete and, as part of the celebration, a large flashing beacon was hoisted to the top. When finished, the Triangle Building, with its shimmering chrome-glass walls, would dominate the park and provide over 250,000 square feet of office space. It would be the largest building ever erected in Atlanta outside of the downtown district and was destined to become one of the most distinctive structures ever built in Georgia.

When construction on it began, Gray Properties already had an arrangement with the Prudential Company. The insurance giant had agreed to purchase the building when it was finished. But they backed out at the last minute and Dick Gray was faced with the possibility of financial ruin. Prudential refused to consider any sort of compromise and, from the things he'd been told, Gray believed they would try to break him and his company if he attempted to enforce the agreement. Tangling with a huge corporation wasn't something he wanted to do, but he felt he had no choice. If Prudential were allowed to walk away from the agreement, Gray Properties would be left holding a $14 million bag. They filed suit against Prudential for breaching the contract and accused the insurance company of economic intimidation.

The struggle between Prudential and Gray Properties dragged on for two years. In the $11 million settlement, Prudential purchased the Triangle Building, then leased it to an investment group called MLN, Inc. Gray Properties then leased the building from that group and finally began renting out the office space. In less than a year, the building was full. It seemed that everybody now wanted to be in the unique, gleaming triangle.

When the promised Century Center Motor Inn was finally opened, it was worth the wait. Built on a triangular floor plan around a 14 story air-conditioned courtyard, there were 299 guestrooms. The hotel boasted a railroad motif and the interior decorations, not the least of which were huge photographic blow-ups of old steam engines, reflected that theme. One of the hotel restaurants was even called the Twentieth Century Limited. It quickly became the favorite convention and meeting center for northeast Atlanta. By the late 1970's Century Center Office Park was a thriving part of the Atlanta business community.

§♢

Life fell into a comfortable routine for Bessie Fisher and the Crums. So much of Remer's time was spent dealing with Century Center that he found it necessary to scale down his own individual business interests. In spite of the increased demands on his time, he was still able to find time for his growing interest in gardening. He seemed to be able to grow any kind of plant. Their yard had the lush appearance of a formal garden and Remer was forever sharing cuttings and rooting new plants.

Emily's involvement with her church and the Embroiderers Guild continued. She also spent considerable time each week on correspondence. She was the sort of woman who not only made friends easily, but kept most of them for life. She corresponded with people all over the world.

The Crums loved to travel. They made numerous trips over the years to places as close as Florida and as far away as Europe. In 1980, they traveled farther than they'd ever been before—to New Zealand. It was the trip of a lifetime and they made the most of it. On the South Island, they hiked into the bush with four other friends and panned for gold. Although a few of the group found a flake or two, Emily was the only one who found a real gold nugget. She was as excited as if she'd won the lottery. The guide, who had been won over by her charm within two minutes of meeting her, pretended to lose the nugget when he transferred it from the pan to a small bottle for her.

She glared at him in mock ferocity. "I'll shoot you!" Then burst out laughing. He handed over her prize with a grin.

§

Emily spoke by phone with her mother every day and usually saw her at least every other day. Bessie often joined the Crums for lunch or dinner and she and Emily enjoyed shopping together. Their favorite store was Lord and Taylor's at Phipps Plaza where they were such regular customers that several of the clerks knew them by name.

Although she spent a lot of time with them, her family was not privy to all of Bessie's comings and goings. That fact was brought home to Emily when she heard this story. In the late seventies, Jane Canipe, daughter of a good friend of the Crums, took a job as a teller in a small bank across the street from Phipps Plaza in Buckhead. On her first day at work, her fellow employees began telling her about their favorite customer—a wonderful little woman who came in the bank every week.

"She's just darling," the teller next to Jane said. "She's always asking about our families and giving us things and doing things for us."

"That's right," a second teller agreed. "One day it started to rain while she was here, so I drove her home. When we got there, she told me to wait. She went upstairs and then brought me a big jar of jelly she had made."

Jane agreed that the woman sounded like a lovely person and looked forward to meeting her.

A few days later, Remer and Bessie walked into the bank. Jane hurried out from behind the counter to greet them and give each of them a hug. After their banking business was concluded, Remer and his mother-in-law left.

"That was her!" a coworker exclaimed. "That's the little lady we've been talking about. How do *you* know her?"

Jane laughed. "I've known her since I was a baby. Her daughter and my mama are best friends."

Emily worried about Bessie living alone. She had tried several times over the years to persuade her mother to move in with her and Remer, but Bessie wouldn't hear of it. She also refused to hire a live-in companion. She was a woman who valued her independence and privacy. However, that attitude had to change when, in early 1981, Bessie fell and broke her hip. Once released from the hospital, she had no choice but to allow a stranger into her home to help with the chores of daily living.

The two women Emily found to share the job of Bessie's caretaker may have started out as strangers, but they quickly became much more than that. Their concern and genuine caring for Bessie, coupled with terrific positive outlooks, quickly earned them places as friends of the whole family.

Bessie's vitality was beginning to dim and Emily was afraid her mother's health might be failing. Bessie recognized her daughter's fear and she tried to comfort her.

"Emily, remember this. When I am ready to go to my heavenly home, an angel will come and tap me on the shoulder and take me into the presence of my Lord. Do not do anything to try and stop this."

"Mother, don't talk like that," Emily protested.

"No. You must listen to me. I want you to remember what I've told you."

And Emily did remember. A few weeks later she called her mother's apartment as she did every morning. When the companion answered, Emily explained she would not be over until the afternoon.

"I have a meeting this morning, Christine. Will you let Mother know?"

"Just a minute. I'll let you tell her yourself. She's had her bath and her breakfast and now she's watching the news on TV."

Christine put down the telephone, but was back in only a few seconds.

"Oh, Emily! She's just dropped off to sleep and I can't wake her!"

The angel had tapped Bessie Ayers Fisher on the shoulder. When she died on February 10, 1982, she was 91 years old.

TWELVE

GIVING BACK

The Crums loved having people in their home. They were always hosting meals or parties for family or friends from their church and service organizations. Their gatherings weren't lavish, but they were always fun and the food was never less than delicious. Remer was reputed to grill the best steak in Georgia and Emily always added inventive touches that made each occasion memorable. Every Fourth of July, everyone they knew was invited to a picnic at their lake cabin in Gwinnett County. There was always plenty of good food and the guests looked forward to the big, cool slices of watermelon that were served in the late afternoon.

Remer and Emily had always tried to give back to the community. Active in their church, they were also involved in a number of other worthwhile organizations. Emily was a long-time member of the Embroiderers Guild and regularly took part in their charitable work. Remer was a member of the American Society of Civil Engineers and gave freely of his time and energy to the Downtown Atlanta Senior Services and the Vinings Improvement and Preservation Association. Still they wanted to do more and, in 1983, they decided on a course of action.

Charles Hudson was a well-known businessman in LaGrange. Founder and owner of a successful insurance agency, he also served as a trustee of the Callaway Foundation and was president of the

LaGrange College Board of Trustees. One summer afternoon in 1983, he took a telephone call in his office.

"Are you the Charles Hudson that has something to do with LaGrange College?" a deep male voice asked.

"Yes, I serve on the Board of Trustees."

"Then you're the Charles Hudson I want. My wife is Emily Fisher Crum and I am Remer Crum. We want to talk to you about giving some land to the college."

"I know who you are." Hudson had grown up in LaGrange and he could still picture Orr Fisher standing outside his auto dealership. As a boy, he had taken speech lessons from Emily. He laughed. "You're the Remer Crum who came to LaGrange and married Emily!"

A few days later, Hudson and the president of LaGrange College traveled to Atlanta and to meet with the Crums in their home. From that meeting came the Emily Fisher Crum Scholarship Fund. The Crums presented the college with a gift of cash and land valued at over $400,000 to be used for scholarships for deserving students. The land they donated was the 370-acre farm Orr and Bessie Fisher had owned just outside of town.

LaGrange College kept the property intact. Periodically the timber from it was harvested and the proceeds went to fund scholarships. At Charles Hudson's suggestion, a large sign was erected on the land facing the main road into town. The sign read, "Growing Scholarships for LaGrange College" and credited Emily and Remer Crum with the gift.

The Crums weren't finished with their giving. One day in early 1984, they were on their way to visit family in Cordele, driving south on Interstate 75. As they passed the small town of Forsyth, they noticed the neat brick buildings and rolling lawns of Tift College spread out to their right. Tift was a Baptist women's college and it seemed to Emily to provide the perfect way to honor her mother's devotion to the Baptist Church. The following year, they endowed the Bessie Ayers Fisher Scholarship Fund at Tift College. As a result of their generosity and interest in the institution, Remer was offered and accepted a position as a trustee of the school.

Founded in 1849, Tift College for Women had been a thriving school for over a hundred years, but competitive recruitment pressure and economic restraints had caused its enrollment to gradually decline to just over 100 students in 1985. The following year it merged with Mercer, a Baptist university in the nearby city of Macon. Mercer offered teaching positions to Tift's entire tenured faculty and absorbed the smaller school's endowment resources, including the Bessie Ayers Fisher Scholarship Fund. To provide a continuity that would assist with the merger, Mercer's trustees wanted to bring several Tift trustees onto their board. Remer Crum was one of those they approached and, 1986, he became a member of Mercer's board of trustees.

Emily and Remer formed a real affinity for Mercer in a very short while. As the months and years passed, they became more and more involved in the life of the school. Remer attended the board meetings regularly and they rarely missed any of the University's special events.

§

In 1984, Emily and Remer bought a condominium in New Smyrna Beach, Florida. Remer especially loved the water. There was nothing he enjoyed more than swimming in the surf. Even when no one else wanted to venture into the water, he would wade out beyond the breakers to swim in the warm Atlantic. When he wasn't in the water, he could usually be found close to it. Early in the morning or late at night, he'd walk for miles along the beach. Suzanne Crum—now a married mother named Suzanne Harper—often visited them and would walk with him. She loved talking with her quiet, intelligent uncle. He seemed to have some knowledge about nearly everything and was willing to share it with her.

The condo was a pleasant, airy place where the Crums vacationed several times a year. They often entertained friends and relatives there and were generous in letting those same people make use of the place when they weren't present.

Suzanne Harper and her family were delighted to accept Emily and Remer's offer for using the condo and tried to make at least one trip a year. It was on one of these visits that Suzanne encountered a pleasant woman beside the pool. The woman held an infant in her arms.

"What is your baby's name?" Suzanne asked.

"Emily."

"Oh, that's my daughter's name, too," she said, indicating her own little girl splashing in the shallow end of the pool. "How did you happen to choose that name?"

The woman smiled. "We named her after a woman we met here. They are the nicest people—from Atlanta. She's just the epitome of a southern lady. I don't think she's here right now. I haven't seen her this week. But her unit's right up there."

She pointed to a fourth-floor apartment—the same apartment where Suzanne and her family were staying.

"You don't mean Emily Crum? That's the same Emily *my* daughter is named for. She's my aunt!"

ℰ

Emily and Remer were married on February 11, 1939. Fifty years to the day later, they renewed their vows at St. Mark United Methodist Church in Atlanta. All but one member of the original wedding party was present in the big church. This time, Remer was unafraid. In fact his face was a study in happy confidence. Emily, dressed in a pale pink silk suit, glowed with joy. When they stood at the altar to reaffirm their vows, the minister, Dr. Lawrence McCullough, asked that all the members of the wedding party and the couple's godchildren and their parents come to the altar as well.

Then he asked Remer, "Do you reaffirm your vows to this woman as your wedded wife and do you promise before God to continue to love her, comfort her, honor and keep her in sickness and health, so long as you both shall live?"

"I do."

Next it was Emily's turn.

"Do you reaffirm your vows to this man as your wedded husband and do you promise before God to continue to love him, comfort him, honor and keep him in sickness and health, so long as you both shall live?"

"I do."

Before the ceremony ended, the Crums presented the church with a wedding kneeler, delicately embroidered with hearts, flowers, a cross, a Bible and wedding bells.

"Worked by me in honor of Remer," Emily told the congregation, "and dedicated to the glory of God."

"To be set apart with thanksgiving, for use in future weddings in Christ's Holy Church," Remer said.

Together they said, "May those who kneel upon it enjoy a full and happy life, in keeping with God's Holy Ordinance."

The Hawaiian Wedding Song was played as they walked back down the aisle.

The service was followed by a reception at the church, hosted by the godchildren and their parents. The celebration continued at the Crums' home afterwards. Friends and family from all over the world had come to share the happy occasion with them. Cards and congratulations poured in, including notes from President George Bush and Georgia Governor Zell Miller. Suzanne Harper and Letsa Marietta had prepared a special surprise for their aunt and uncle. Each invitation to the party had been accompanied by a request for mementos and memories of Emily and Remer's life together. Friends and family members had replied with stories, photos and souvenirs. All the responses were placed in a scrapbook and presented to the couple.

Grover C. Hunter, Jr. had attended LaGrange High School with Emily Fisher. He had gone on to become a noted educator and poet and, in honor of their special day, he wrote the following poem:

For Emily and Remer
On Their Fiftieth Wedding Anniversary

Candles by the altar burn
As brightly now as fifty years ago.
The vows you spoke in youth
Still stand in autumn's afterglow!

I remember well the dream –
Our little band set out one day
On a journey through the wild.
Alas, some schoolmates snatched along the way!

Though now our ranks are lean,
The tie that binds you ever
Affirms the spirit of our class
We yet march on as one together!

We who are left rejoice in song
On your anniversary of gold.
May all your days be candle-lighted
With memories to cherish and to hold!

The apple orchard Remer planted in 1963 produced wonderful fruit year after year. In the late sixties, he and Emily put ads in the newspaper advertising "pick your own apples" for one or two weekends each fall. They would go out to the cabin and set up their scales. As people came and picked the apples, they would bring them to Remer. He'd take them, weigh them and take the money. However, no one was ever charged for the fruit they ate while they were picking it off the trees.

Eventually Emily and Remer began harvesting their own crop. They'd pull bushel after bushel of fruit from the trees. Remer would fill the bed of his pick up truck and sit on the side of Five Forks Road and sell baskets of apples. Later he developed regular routes. Every October, he would deliver his apples to many of the private schools in Atlanta. Lovett and Westminster were two of his best customers.

But, in 1998, they sold the orchard and lake property in Gwinnett County. When he was asked why, Remer laughed. "Every year the trees got bigger and I got older and, when those two paths crossed, that was the end of it."

Thirteen

A Vision Realized

In the year 2000, the world seemed obsessed with the 21st century and all it held for humanity. Everyone was looking forward and the Crums were no exception. Content with their life and circumstances, they still had concerns about the future. Theirs was a sizable estate—the Century Center property being the most significant piece. They wanted to be sure it would eventually go to benefit the cause that had been theirs for so many years—education. They struggled to decide the best way to accomplish that goal. They could establish a trust, they knew, but they weren't convinced that would be right for them.

"You know, the administrators or trustees of your estate don't always do what you would like done," Remer said. "That happens so often. They get arbitrary among themselves or don't see what you wanted. It's an asset that, if not handled right, might be a liability somewhere down the line. The trustees might not have the time to fool with it. They might decide to divide it up and sell it."

Emily knew he was right. She was also very concerned that the Century Center property be maintained as a single entity. That was what Orr Fisher had wanted. It was what she and Remer and her mother had worked so hard to keep in place after her father's death. She hated to think it might be split up and sold off in pieces.

They finally decided that the best way to accomplish what they wanted was to ensure that the property go directly to the institutions that would benefit from it. That way they could bypass any question of interference by trustees or estate administrators.

They chose to make Mercer University and LaGrange College equal beneficiaries of the Century Center property under their wills. They were not concerned that one school was affiliated with the Baptist Church and the other with the Methodist Church.

"We thought we'd get them together," Emily joked later.

Before contacting anyone at the schools, the Crums first met with Benjamin White, an attorney at the Alston & Bird law firm, on August 17, 2000. They explained what they wanted to do. Remer laid out exactly how he thought the matter should be handled.

The agreement they asked White to draw up for the transfer of the property to the two colleges would provide that the current ground lease would remain in force and neither school could sell or in any way encumber the property until the expiration of that lease in 2058. It also made it difficult, although not impossible, for the land to be sold after the expiration of the lease. The income generated from the current lease would go to the existing scholarship funds the Crums had already established at the schools. Emily and Remer also wanted to change the names of those funds. The Emily Fisher Crum Fund at LaGrange College would now be known as the Emily and Remer Crum Fund. The Bessie Ayers Fisher Fund at Mercer University would have its name changed to the Thomas Orr and Bessie Ayers Fisher Memorial Endowed Scholarship Fund.

"We'd like to have the final closing on the agreement some time in October," Remer told him.

White assured him he would handle everything. It took only a few weeks for all the paperwork to be assembled and approved by his clients. Then on September 21st White sent the presidents of both schools a letter explaining the gift the Crums planned to donate to their institutions. He asked that they meet with him and the Crums in his office on October 11th. He was not surprised when he received almost immediate notice that they would be present on that day.

The meeting began promptly at 2:00 o'clock that October afternoon. Remer was preoccupied with the details, concerned that everything that needed to be covered would be. Emily was just excited. She loved giving gifts and this was the best one yet. They took their seats around the shiny table in one of the firm's conference rooms. Vice President and General Counsel, Bill Solomon, and Senior Vice President of Advancement, Emily Myers, accompanied Mercer University President Kirby Godsey. LaGrange President Stuart Gulley brought his Vice President of Advancement, David Rowe, and Legal Counsel, Daniel Lee, with him.

While Benjamin White began by making the introductions, it was Remer Crum's meeting from the start. He laid it all out for them—the property, its potential income and appraised value. He wanted to be sure they understood his and Emily's concern that the land remained intact. Emily shared some memories of the farm with them, hoping to make everyone understand why it was such a special place to her and her family. Then it was time. The agreements were passed around the table and signed by the parties. The gift was now official.

Emily and Remer prepared to leave, but President Gulley stopped them. He said that he and President Godsey would like to do something for them, to recognize them in some way for what they were doing for the schools. It was clear from the expressions on their faces that the Crums never expected any sort of formal recognition of their gift during their lifetimes.

"Oh, I don't think that's really necessary," Remer said.

But the others were adamant.

"We really believe that you deserve to be recognized and celebrated for what you're doing," President Godsey said. "Your gift is significant enough that I think it could serve as a model for what others might do."

That got Remer's attention. He knew there were other people out there with the capacity to do something like this to further higher education. If his and Emily's gift might inspire similar ones, then he was all for the public recognition. They agreed that a luncheon in their honor would be fine.

The weeks leading up to the luncheon were busy for the staffs of both schools. There were press releases to be prepared, invitations to be issued and the meal to be planned. Dean Hartman, Director of Public Relations for LaGrange College, arranged for aerial photos to be made of Century Center Park. But when the prints were sent to him, he had a hard time determining what was part of the office park and what wasn't. So much commercial development had arisen around the land since 1969 that it was almost impossible to determine the park's boundaries. At least, it was almost impossible for Dean Hartman. When he sat down with Remer Crum a week later, that gentleman had no difficulty in discerning the boundaries of the land he knew so well.

"Now," he said, "starting with the creek here . . ."

In no time at all, the boundaries of the park were marked on the photos.

On December 21st, the luncheon honoring Emily and Remer was held at the Capital City Club in downtown Atlanta. It was a sparkling affair with a high-powered guest list, but there was no doubt as to who were the stars of the occasion. Emily and Remer were the center of attention from the first minute forward.

Presidents Godsey and Gulley each addressed the gathering. They thanked the Crums for their incredible generosity and then unveiled a large aerial photograph on which the boundaries of Century Center had been prominently marked. A brief biography of each guest of honor was presented.

When Stuart Gulley mentioned that Emily had been a teacher in LaGrange, he said, "In fact, we have here today one of her former students in Charles Hudson. Charles, can you by any chance remember any of the speeches that Emily taught you?"

Hudson was sitting right beside Emily. He got to his feet without a trace of embarrassment. "I certainly can." He then recited a few lines that began "I'm proud to be an American", to the obvious delight of his former teacher. The audience erupted with applause.

The Crums were then asked to come forward for a series of photographs, but Emily, bursting with joy, wanted to share her feelings with those people gathered there. She crossed to the podium and told them how special the day was for her. She placed a photo of her parents beside the big aerial picture and explained how Orr and Bessie Fisher had kept the property for so many years. "They are really the ones responsible for this gift."

Her husband followed her at the podium. Remer thanked them for the luncheon and reiterated his and Emily's desire that the property not be sold. With a grin, he told the two college presidents, "I'll be up in heaven looking down on you to make sure you don't sell it."

The Crums were honored in other ways during the coming year, although they weren't always aware that these honors were coming their way. In April, they attended the Mercer Trustees meeting at Sea Island, Georgia. They had been participants at many such meetings over the years and thought nothing of it. Dinner on Saturday night was held at The Cloister. When Emily and Remer arrived, they checked in at the door for the usual nametags and seating assignments.

"Mr. and Mrs. Crum, you're at table number one."

They made their way through the dining room, stopping to greet friends and exchange pleasantries. No one was yet seated when they found their assigned table, but Emily pulled out one of the chairs so she could put down her purse. The programs for the evening had been placed in the seats of the chairs and, as Emily glanced down, she noticed that the woman pictured on the front of the program wore a dress that was similar to one she owned herself. She'd even considered wearing that dress this evening and was now relieved that she'd chosen another. Then, looking more closely, she realized the photo on the front of the program was of her and Remer, taken at the winter President's Club meeting. That was her first indication they were to be honored here as well.

At Mercer's May 13, 2001 Commencement, Emily and Remer Crum were awarded honorary degrees. Remer received the doctor of law degree and Emily received the doctor of humanities degree.

"Thanks to you," President Godsey told them during the ceremony, "generations of students will leave Mercer's halls to make important and enduring contributions."

LaGrange College bestowed honorary degrees on the Crums during their May 2002 Commencement.

Although they have enjoyed the celebrations and the honors, Emily and Remer understand that the significance of their gift may not be fully realized for decades. "It's going to take time and thought and vision for the future trustees to decide how they will handle the property when the lease expires," Remer said.

According to Stuart Gulley, "It is the kind of gift that a president can only dream about getting and very few are blessed to receive. When the ground leases mature, I can only imagine what might happen. That's 57 years from now. I'm sure there are going to be a lot of buildings on campus that may need some renovating and improving. There are no doubt going to be buildings that still need to be built. But however it's used, it will be a transforming gift."

Kirby Godsey also speculated on the future with respect to the Crums' gift. "When the leases do run out, the re-negotiation will be immensely important. I think everybody knows they are so undervalued at this point. But until that time, the priority here will be giving scholarships that recognize the Crums. Emily and Remer Crum are never going to be lost in the history of this institution."

The Crums never forget the origins of their gift. Remer observed, "Way back then, people unknowingly planted the seeds by being frugal, honest and forthright. Nancy Hemphill could never have dreamed that her small bequest would be the beginning of something like this. It has continued through the generations due to the sacrifices made. We are only putting into effect the dreams of Emily's mother and father. They held onto the land instead of spending money on themselves. Now it will be something really important to two colleges and many, many boys and girls."

President Godsey is pleased that Mercer University Press will be publishing this book. "People will want to hear about the Crums—people who will benefit from their generosity and their grace, but didn't have the pleasure of knowing them."

For those of us who have had the pleasure of knowing Emily and Remer Crum, that knowledge is the real gift.

EMILY FISHER CRUM'S BOOK OF INSTRUCTIONS

The following five pages are samples of Emily Fisher Crum's Book of Instructions which she wrote; the art was supplied by a staff artist.

The
PEARL HARBOR
NAVY YARD

★

Sends Aloha
to you. We hope the
few suggestions
we are able to off-
er will be helpful
to you on your
journey out.

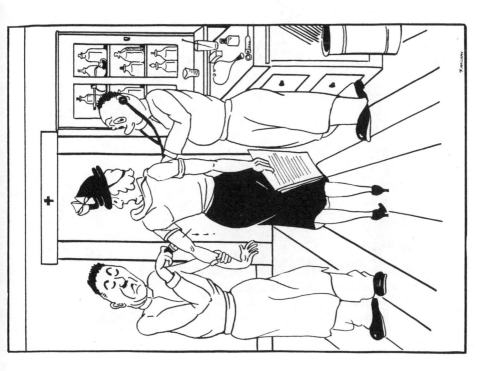

You will arrive in Crockett, Oakland or San Francisco, California.

From Crockett you take a bus, which you catch at the railroad station, to Vallejo, California. If it is Sunday when you arrive in Vallejo take a taxi to the "Girls' Dormitory," and remain there until Monday morning, then report to the office outside the main gate at Mare Island.

From Oakland take a train into San Francisco and go from the station to the Mare Island Personnel Branch Office in the Ferry Building.

You will be told at the Ferry Building when to report to the Labor Board at Mare Island. You will ask for the Pearl Harbor Section.

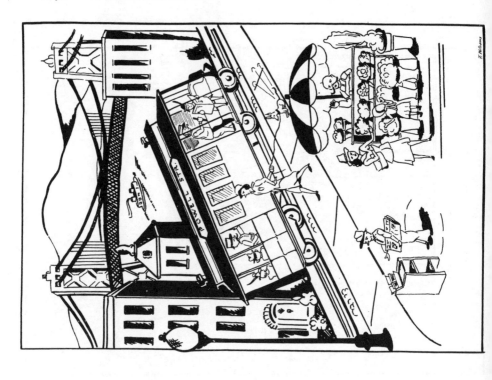

You will remain in San Francisco from twenty four hours to Six weeks. Be sure to have a coat and a few warm dresses to wear while in San Francisco. The weather is very cool there at times.

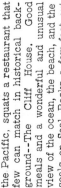

Perched on a cliff, above the surf of the Pacific, squats a restaurant that few can match in historical background--The Cliff House. Good meals and a wonderful and unusual view of the ocean, the beach, and the seals on Seal Rocks a few feet out from the shore. Don't miss their picture gallery in the lobby as you go in. Probably one of the finest collections of autographed pictures of far famed people in existence, from the President to Clark Gable. This is also the place where "Alexander's Rag Time Band" had it's first performance.

For the devotees of French food Francois Ripley's is the place to go. Served on long tables by buxom French lassies, their meals are grand and cost only $1.25. A real French restaurant with a real French atmosphere.

The cable cars in San Francisco are the world's first and will probably be the world's last as the city loves them still. Probably the most interesting route is the O'Farrell Street car ride.

At the end of the Powell Street cable line lies Fisherman's Wharf. Immortalized in pictures and books it will always be a mecca for the lovers of sea foods. You won't go wrong on any of the restaurants that line the wharf, but one that is especially well known is the Fisherman's Grotto. A trip to the "Grotto" minus their Crab Chapino is like a trip to Niagara without seeing the Falls. They will bring you a little apron that you will be very glad to use because there is only one way to eat Chapino--with the hands.

DOCUMENTS PERTAINING TO THE CENTURY CENTER

The following 18 pages are photo-reproductions of official documents relating to the gift of the Century Center to LaGrange College and Mercer University.

STATEMENT OF INTENTIONS

This document represents a Statement Of Intentions
between EMILY F. CRUM and REMER H. CRUM, Owners of Century
Center Office Park, parties of the First Part, and F.
Stuart Gulley, President of LaGrange College, LaGrange,
Georgia and R. Kirby Godsey, President of Mercer University,
Macon, Georgia, parties of the Second Part regards the
Owner's desire to bequeath the Owner's interest in the
Leased Fee in the Eighty-Three and Thirty-Five One Hundredth
(83.35) acre Office Park identified as Century Center Office
Park, located between Clairmont Road and Interstate I-85 in
Dekalb County, Georgia.

THIS STATEMENT OF INTENTIONS is agreed to by both the
parties of the First Part and parties of the Second Part
subject to the following provisions:

1. The parties of the First Part intend to bequeath
the subject property to the parties of the SEcond Part in
equal amounts.

2. The parties of the First Part will continue to
own and manage the Leased Fee during the life times of either
and/or both of the parties of the First Part. The Leased Fee
is subject to a long term ground lease and will not mature
until December 31, 2058.

3. After the subject property has been bequeathed to
the parties of the Second Part, the Leased Fee will become
owned and must be managed by the parties of the Second
Part and the parties of the Second Part may wish to engage
an agent to manage the subject property subject to direction
of the parties of the Second Part.

4. The parties of the Second Part agree that the subject property will not be mortgaged,sold or otherwise encumbered by the parties of the Second Part during the life time of the Lease.

5. After the Lease maturity date of December 31, 2058 the parties of the Second Part may sell the total property in one single transaction ONLY and the net proceeds of the sale be equally divided between the parties of the Second Part, and these equal amounts of sale proceeds will be deposited in either ONE or BOTH of the following accounts:

      A.Existing Scholarship Accounts presently established at LaGrange College and Mercer University.

      B.Capital Improvement Accounts at LaGrange College and Mercer University.

      6. It is the wish of the parties of the First Part that any relative of either Emily F. Crum and/ or Remer H. Crum be given special consideration for financial assistance when they may be seeking student admission and/or student aid..

ALSTON&BIRD LLP

One Atlantic Center
1201 West Peachtree Street
Atlanta, Georgia 30309-3424

404-881-7000
Fax: 404-881-7777
www.alston.com

Benjamin T. White   Direct Dial: 404-881-7488   E-mail: bwhite@alston.com

September 21, 2000

President F. Stuart Gulley
LaGrange College
601 Broad Street
LaGrange, Georgia 30240-2999

President R. Kirby Godsey
Mercer University
1400 Coleman Avenue
Macon, Georgia 31207-0001

> Re: **Mr. and Mrs. Remer H. Crum**
>   **Proposed Gifts to LaGrange College and Mercer University**

Gentlemen:

Our clients Emily Fisher Crum and Remer H. Crum propose to leave their entire interest in Century Center Office Park in equal shares to LaGrange College and Mercer University. They anticipate that these gifts will be made when the survivor of them dies.

Enclosed are the following three agreements:

1.   **Agreement with LaGrange College for the Creation and Administration of the Emily Fisher Crum Fund.** This agreement is intended to clarify the terms of the Emily Fisher Crum Fund at LaGrange College.

2.   **Agreement with Mercer University for the Creation and Administration of the Bessie Ayers Fisher Memorial Endowed Scholarship Fund.** This agreement is intended to clarify the terms of the Bessie Ayers Fisher Memorial Endowed Scholarship Fund at Mercer University.

3.   **Agreement with Mercer University and LaGrange College Pertaining to Century Center Office Park.** This agreement sets out the terms of Mr. and Mrs.

President F. Stuart Gulley
LaGrange College
President R. Kirby Godsey
Mercer University
September 21, 2000
Page 2

Crum's proposed gifts of their interest in Century Center Office Park to LaGrange College and Mercer University.

I will appreciate your reviewing these agreements and letting me have your comments by October 5, 2000, if possible. Mr. and Mrs. Crum and I will be glad to consider any changes to the agreements you and your attorneys think would improve them. Since these agreements will remain in effect for quite some time, in perpetuity in the case of the scholarship funds, we want to be certain they will carry out Mr. and Mrs. Crum's and your intent.

Mr. and Mrs. Crum would like to close these gift transactions by having the final versions of the three agreements signed in our offices at 2:00 p.m. on Wednesday, October 11, 2000. Therefore, we will appreciate an early response from you.

With kindest regards.

Sincerely,

Benjamin T. White

BTW:ar
Enclosures
cc: Mr. and Mrs. Remer H. Crum (without enclosures)
ATL01/10824786v1

MERCER UNIVERSITY
SCHOOL OF EDUCATION
COLLEGE OF LIBERAL ARTS

AGREEMENT BETWEEN EMILY FISHER CRUM, REMER H. CRUM,
AND THE CORPORATION OF MERCER UNIVERSITY
FOR THE CREATION AND ADMINISTRATION OF
THE THOMAS ORR AND BESSIE AYERS FISHER
MEMORIAL ENDOWED SCHOLARSHIP FUND

THIS AGREEMENT ("Agreement") is made as of the 11th day of October, 2000, between EMILY FISHER CRUM and REMER H. CRUM, individual residents of the State of Georgia ("Donors"), and THE CORPORATION OF MERCER UNIVERSITY, an educational institution located in the State of Georgia ("Mercer University"). The purpose of this Agreement is to confirm the terms of the creation and administration of a scholarship fund, to be renamed the Thomas Orr and Bessie Ayers Fisher Memorial Endowed Scholarship Fund ("Fund"), which the Donors created in 1984 for the benefit of Tift College, which subsequently was merged into Mercer University. All persons and organizations making contributions to the Fund shall be bound by the terms of this Agreement.

1. **Introduction.**

(a) The Donors wish to encourage and support education at Mercer University, particularly in the School of Education and College of Liberal Arts at Mercer University, through the Thomas Orr and Bessie Ayers Fisher Memorial Endowed Scholarship Fund. The purpose of the Fund is to provide scholarships to students who are studying either in the School of Education or in the College of Liberal Arts at Mercer University.

(b) Mercer University is a tax-exempt public charity described in sections 501(c)(3) and 509(a)(1) of the Internal Revenue Code, as amended, and is an appropriate organization to hold and administer the Fund for the purposes described in this Agreement.

(c) The creation and administration of the Fund is entirely consistent with the charitable and educational purposes and functions of Mercer University.

2.   **Name of Fund.**

The name of the Fund created hereby is: THE THOMAS ORR AND BESSIE AYERS FISHER MEMORIAL ENDOWED SCHOLARSHIP FUND. Any recipient of benefits from this Fund shall be advised that such benefits are from the Thomas Orr and Bessie Ayers Fisher Memorial Endowed Scholarship Fund.

3.   **Contributions to Mercer University.**

The Donors have made, and may continue to make during their lifetimes and/or at their deaths, contributions to the Fund. Mercer University agrees that it will hold and administer all amounts contributed to the Fund for the purposes and uses and on the terms and conditions set forth in this Agreement.

4.   **Purpose.**

The purpose of this Fund is to provide full or partial scholarships each year to assist deserving students enrolled either in the School of Education or in the College of Liberal Arts at Mercer University. It is the Donors' intention that scholarships from this Fund will be used to defray the costs of education in the School of Education and in the College of Liberal Arts at Mercer University, including tuition, fees, and other related expenses and charges.

5.   **Procedures.**

(a)   The assets of the Fund shall be invested as the governing body of Mercer University deems best, and distributions from the Fund shall be made each year in accordance with such spending policies for the Fund as the governing body of Mercer University shall adopt from time to time. It is the Donors' intention that this Fund will be held and administered as an endowment fund to carry out the purposes provided for in this Agreement in perpetuity, and the Donors request that distributions from the Fund each year not exceed five percent (5%) of the average of the fair market values of the assets of the Fund as of the close of the last business day of each of the Fund's three previous years. However, the Donors authorize the Chief Executive Officer and the Board of Trustees of Mercer University to exceed the five percent (5%) spending limitation described above if they jointly determine that it would further the purposes of the Fund and the Donors' intent in creating the Fund to do so.

(b)   One-half (1/2) of amounts distributed from the Fund each year shall be used to award full or partial scholarships to students enrolled in the School of Education at Mercer University, and one-half (1/2) of amounts distributed from the Fund each year shall be used to provide full or partial scholarships to students enrolled in the College of Liberal Arts at Mercer University. In selecting the recipient or recipients of the scholarships under this Agreement, consideration shall be given to such factors as academic achievement, financial need, and other similar factors, and to recommendations

- 2 -

of the Donors. The number of scholarships awarded and the amount of each scholarship hereunder shall be determined by the Board of Trustees of Mercer University in its discretion.

(c)   The Donors hope, but they do not direct, that in awarding scholarships under this Agreement Mercer University will give special consideration to the descendants of either Donor's grandparents.

6.   Additions to the Fund.

Additions of property which are so designated and which are acceptable to Mercer University shall be set aside as a part of the Fund, provided that all such additions by whomever made shall be held, administered, and disbursed under the same terms and conditions as set forth in this Agreement, as if such property had originally been a part of the Fund.

7.   Successor Organizations.

Whenever Mercer University is named or referred to herein, it shall be deemed to include successors thereto.

8.   Power of Modification.

(a)   While either Donor is living, this Agreement may be amended by mutual agreement in writing of the Donor(s) and Mercer University.

(b)   When neither Donor is living, if at any time, in the judgment of the Board of Trustees of Mercer University, the uses and purposes of the Fund as described above become, in effect, unnecessary, impracticable, or incapable of fulfillment, then the Fund held under this Agreement may be held, administered, and distributed for such other purposes as the Board of Trustees of Mercer University in its discretion shall determine, giving consideration to the Donors' special interest in financial aid to students enrolled in the School of Education and the College of Liberal Arts at Mercer University.

IN WITNESS WHEREOF, the Donors and Mercer University have executed this Agreement, as of the day and year first above written.

DONORS:

EMILY FISHER CRUM

_____ [SEAL]

Witness

- 3 -

REMER H. CRUM

Remer H. Crum [SEAL]

Benjamin T. White
Witness

THE CORPORATION OF MERCER UNIVERSITY

By: _____
Authorized Officer

ATTEST: _____
Authorized Officer

Benjamin T. White
Witness

[CORPORATE SEAL]

AGREEMENT BETWEEN EMILY FISHER CRUM, REMER H. CRUM, LAGRANGE COLLEGE, AND THE CORPORATION OF MERCER UNIVERSITY PERTAINING TO CENTURY CENTER OFFICE PARK

THIS AGREEMENT ("Agreement") is made as of the 11th day of October, 2000, in Atlanta, Georgia.

THE PARTIES to it are EMILY FISHER CRUM, REMER H. CRUM, LAGRANGE COLLEGE ("LaGrange College"), and THE CORPORATION OF MERCER UNIVERSITY ("Mercer University"). Emily Fisher Crum and Remer H. Crum may be referred to in this Agreement individually as the "Donor" and together as the "Donors."

THE BACKGROUND of this Agreement is as follows:

1.   The Donors own real estate consisting of an 83.35 acre office park identified as Century Center Office Park, located between Clairmont Road and Interstate I-85 in DeKalb County, Georgia ("Property"). The Property is subject to a long term ground lease the term of which runs until December 31, 2058.

2.   The Donors presently intend to contribute their entire interest in the Property in equal shares to LaGrange College and Mercer University, subject to the terms and conditions of this Agreement. In no event, however, shall this Agreement create a legally binding obligation on the part of either Donor to contribute any part of his or her interest in the Property either to LaGrange College or to Mercer University at any time.

3.   LaGrange College and Mercer University each are tax-exempt public charities described in sections 501(c)(3) and 509(a)(1) of the Internal Revenue Code, and each is an appropriate organization to receive, hold, and administer the Donors' interest in the Property for the charitable and educational purposes and functions set forth in this Agreement.

4.   The purpose of this Agreement is to determine and settle the charitable and educational uses and purposes of the Property in the event the Donors contribute their interest in the Property to LaGrange College and Mercer University and the terms and conditions which will govern LaGrange College's and Mercer University's ownership and use of the Property.

THE TERMS of this Agreement are as follows:

1.   **LaGrange College's and Mercer University's Use of the Property During the Term of the Ground Lease.**

(a)   At such time in the future as LaGrange College and Mercer University receive the Donors' interest in the Property (which the Donors anticipate will be at the death of the survivor of them), LaGrange College and Mercer University shall hold, manage, and administer their respective interests in the Property either directly or through one or more agents or other management arrangements as they may deem necessary or desirable.

(b)   During the term of the ground lease to which the Property is subject, that is, until December 31, 2058, LaGrange College and Mercer University agree, jointly and severally, that they will not sell, assign, transfer, give, mortgage, encumber, or otherwise dispose of any part of their interest in the Property unless both LaGrange College and Mercer University jointly determine that there is a compelling reason to do so.

(c)   While LaGrange College and Mercer University hold their respective interests in the Property subject to the ground lease, any net income they derive from their interests in the Property shall be used as follows:

(i)   LaGrange College shall add its share of the net income from the Property to the Emily and Remer Crum Fund, a scholarship fund which the Donors have created at LaGrange College.

(ii)   Mercer University shall add its share of the net income from the Property to the Thomas Orr and Bessie Ayers Fisher Memorial Endowed Scholarship Fund, a scholarship fund which the Donors have created at Mercer University.

2.   **Disposition of the Property After the Termination of the Ground Lease.**

(a)   After the termination of the ground lease to which the Property is now subject, LaGrange College and Mercer University may sell or otherwise dispose of their entire interests in the Property, but not less than their entire interests in the Property; and the net proceeds from any such sale or other disposition of the Property shall be distributed as follows:

(i)   LaGrange College shall add some, all, or none of its share of such proceeds to the Emily and Remer Crum Fund; and any part of its share of such proceeds not added to the Emily and Remer Crum Fund shall be used for capital improvements at LaGrange College, preferably for new school buildings and new school-related facilities in memory of the Donors.

- 2 -

(ii)   Mercer University shall add some, all, or none of its share of such proceeds to the Thomas Orr and Bessie Ayers Fisher Memorial Endowed Scholarship Fund; and any part of its share of such proceeds not added to the Thomas Orr and Bessie Ayers Memorial Endowed Scholarship Fund shall be used for capital improvements at Mercer University, preferably for new school buildings and new school-related facilities in memory of the Donors.

3.   **Power of Modification.**

(a)   While either Donor is living, this Agreement may be amended by mutual agreement in writing of the Donor(s), LaGrange College, and Mercer University.

(b)   When neither Donor is living, if at any time the governing bodies of LaGrange College and Mercer University jointly determine that any provision of this Agreement has become unnecessary or impracticable or incapable of fulfillment, the governing bodies of LaGrange College and Mercer University, acting together, may modify such provision but only if any such modification comes as close as possible to carrying out the Donors' original charitable intent as expressed in this Agreement.

4.   **Successor Organizations.** Whenever LaGrange College or Mercer University is named or referred to herein, it shall be deemed to include successors thereto.

IN WITNESS WHEREOF, the Donors, LaGrange College, and Mercer University have executed this Agreement, as of the day and year first shown above.

DONORS:

EMILY FISHER CRUM

_____ [SEAL]

_____
Witness

REMER H. CRUM

_____ [SEAL]

_____
Witness

- 3 -

ATL01/10820026v1

LAGRANGE COLLEGE

By: _____
Authorized Officer

ATTEST: _____
Authorized Officer

Witness

[CORPORATE SEAL]

THE CORPORATION OF MERCER UNIVERSITY

By: _____
Authorized Officer

ATTEST: _____
Authorized Officer

Witness

[CORPORATE SEAL]

- 4 -

LAGRANGE COLLEGE

AGREEMENT BETWEEN EMILY FISHER CRUM, REMER H. CRUM, AND LAGRANGE COLLEGE FOR THE CREATION AND ADMINISTRATION OF THE EMILY AND REMER CRUM FUND

THIS AGREEMENT ("Agreement") is made as of the 11th day of October, 2000, between EMILY FISHER CRUM and REMER H. CRUM, individual residents of the State of Georgia ("Donors"), and LAGRANGE COLLEGE, an educational institution located in LaGrange, Georgia ("LaGrange College"). The purpose of this Agreement is to confirm the terms of the creation and administration of a scholarship fund, to be renamed the Emily and Remer Crum Fund ("Fund"), which the Donors have created for the benefit of LaGrange College. All persons and organizations making contributions to the Fund shall be bound by the terms of this Agreement.

1. **Introduction.**

   (a) The Donors wish to encourage and support education at LaGrange College through the Emily and Remer Crum Fund. The purpose of the Fund is to provide scholarships to students enrolled at LaGrange College.

   (b) LaGrange College is a tax-exempt public charity described in sections 501(c)(3) and 509(a)(1) of the Internal Revenue Code, as amended, and is an appropriate organization to hold and administer the Fund for the purposes described in this Agreement.

   (c) The creation and administration of the Fund is entirely consistent with the charitable and educational purposes and functions of LaGrange College.

2. **Name of Fund.**

   The name of the Fund created hereby is: THE EMILY AND REMER CRUM FUND. Any recipient of benefits from this Fund shall be advised that such benefits are from the Emily and Remer Crum Fund.

3. **Contributions to LaGrange College.**

   The Donors have made, and may continue to make during their lifetimes and/or at their deaths, contributions to the Fund. LaGrange College agrees that it will hold and administer all amounts contributed to the Fund for the purposes and uses and on the terms and conditions set forth in this Agreement.

4.   **Purpose.**

The purpose of this Fund is to provide full or partial scholarships each year to assist deserving students enrolled at LaGrange College. It is the Donors' intention that scholarships from this Fund will be used to defray the costs of education at LaGrange College, including tuition, fees, and other related expenses and charges.

5.   **Procedures.**

(a)   The assets of the Fund shall be invested as the governing body of LaGrange College deems best, and distributions from the Fund shall be made each year in accordance with such spending policies for the Fund as the governing body of LaGrange College shall adopt from time to time. It is the Donors' intention that this Fund will be held and administered as an endowment fund to carry out the purposes provided for in this Agreement in perpetuity, and the Donors request that distributions from the Fund each year not exceed five percent (5%) of the average of the fair market values of the assets of the Fund as of the close of the last business day of each of the Fund's three previous years. However, the Donors authorize the Chief Executive Officer and the Board of Trustees of LaGrange College to exceed the five percent (5%) spending limitation described above if they jointly determine that it would further the purposes of the Fund and the Donors' intent in creating the Fund to do so.

(b)   Full or partial scholarships shall be awarded from the Fund each year to enable students to study at LaGrange College. In selecting the recipient or recipients of the scholarships under this Agreement, consideration shall be given to such factors as academic achievement, financial need, and other similar factors and to recommendations of the Donors. The number of scholarships awarded and the amount of each scholarship hereunder shall be determined by the Board of Trustees of LaGrange College in its discretion.

(c)   The Donors hope, but they do not direct, that in awarding scholarships under this Agreement LaGrange College will give special consideration to the descendants of either Donor's grandparents.

6.   **Additions to the Fund.**

Additions of property which are so designated and which are acceptable to LaGrange College shall be set aside as a part of the Fund, provided that all such additions by whomever made shall be held, administered, and disbursed under the same terms and conditions as set forth in this Agreement, as if such property had originally been a part of the Fund.

7.   **Successor Organizations.**

Whenever LaGrange College is named or referred to herein, it shall be deemed to include successors thereto.

- 2 -

8. **Power of Modification.**

(a)   While either Donor is living, this Agreement may be amended by mutual agreement in writing of the Donor(s) and LaGrange College.

(b)   When neither Donor is living, if at any time, in the judgment of the Board of Trustees of LaGrange College, the uses and purposes of the Fund as described above become, in effect, unnecessary, impracticable, or incapable of fulfillment, then the Fund held under this Agreement may be held, administered, and distributed for such other purposes as the Board of Trustees of LaGrange College in its discretion shall determine.

IN WITNESS WHEREOF, the Donors and LaGrange College have executed this Agreement, as of the day and year first above written.

DONORS:

EMILY FISHER CRUM

_____ [SEAL]
Witness

REMER H. CRUM

_____ [SEAL]
Witness

LAGRANGE COLLEGE

By: _____
Authorized Officer

ATTEST:

_____
Authorized Officer
Witness

[CORPORATE SEAL]

- 3 -

LAGRANGE COLLEGE

601 Broad Street ☐ LaGrange, Georgia 30240-2999

(706) 880-8230   FAX (706) 880-8358
sgulley@lgc.edu

Office of the President

October 12, 2000

Mr. and Mrs. Remer H. Crum
4274 Paces Ferry Road, NW
Atlanta, GA 30339

Dear Remer and Emily:

Yesterday was an historic and memorable day for LaGrange College. Never in my life have I imagined that, as a college president, I would have the opportunity to sit around a table in a lawyer's office with such extraordinary individuals as you to consummate an arrangement that will forever transform LaGrange College for the better.

We have been, of course, very proud of the fact that Emily is one of our graduates, but we never could have imagined what an enormous blessing the two of you would become to this institution and her future. I am deeply grateful to you for what you intend to do to further the work of this college and the students who attend here. Words are simply inadequate to express the profound gratitude that the trustees, faculty, staff, students, and I feel about what you are doing for LaGrange College.

We will be in touch with you in the near future about ways we might recognize publicly your generosity. In the meantime, know that I am so very thankful for the witness the two of you have made in sharing so graciously the abundant resources with which God has blessed you. My prayer is that in return we will use of this gift in such a significant way that from "on high" you will beam with pride at what you are doing for this institution.

All best wishes to you both.

Sincerely yours,

F. Stuart Gulley

FSG/lew

October 13, 2000

Mr. & Mrs. Remer H. Crum
4274 Paces Ferry Road, SE
Atlanta, GA 30339-3782

Dear Remer and Emily:

Words often fail us when we feel such a deep sense of gratitude. Generations of Mercerians will be affected by your generous and thoughtful decision. Countless young people will have an opportunity to go to college where their own lives will be shaped and challenged and they will be enabled to achieve their best and to contribute effectively to their families and communities. It is apparent to all of us that both of you have given caring and careful thought to these decisions. Your willingness to take the long look at the impact of your decisions far beyond any of our lives reflects the highest standards of stewardship and personal responsibility.

I look forward to occasions to learn about this property which you have managed with such great care. My colleagues and I want to learn from you and your experience so that our own decisions in subsequent years will be informed by the experience and choices you have made.

While being sensitive to your own desires will be foremost, the University and especially the Board of Trustees will want to convey in continuing ways both our appreciation for your generous decision and our joy for the enduring difference you are making in the future of Mercer University. Mercer University and the legacy of Tift College will be perpetually strengthened and undergirded by your spirit and your actions.

On behalf of all my colleagues I am grateful for your generous gift, your personal grace, and your special friendship.

Sincerely yours,

R. Kirby Godsey
President

rkg:db

cc: Emily P. Myers
        William G. Solomon, IV

INDEX